Are We There Yet?

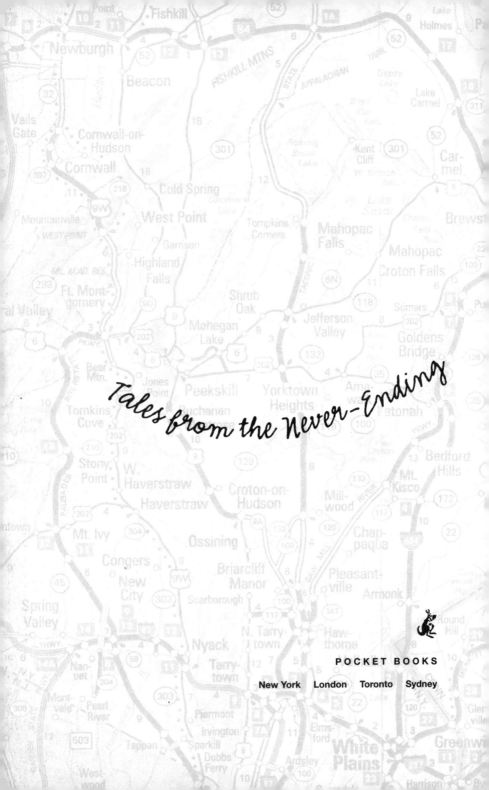

Tales from the Never-Ending

POCKET BOOKS

New York London Toronto Sydney

Are We There Yet?

Travels of WWE Superstars

Robert Caprio

World
Wrestling
Entertainment®

POCKET BOOKS, a division of Simon & Schuster, Inc.
1230 Avenue of the Americas. New York, NY 10020

Photos on pages 22, 64, 165 courtesy of Molly Holly.
Photo on page 18 courtesy of Dr. Tom Prichard. Photos on
pages 58, 69, 110, 135 courtesy of Ivory. Photo on page 90
courtesy of D-Von Dudley.

ISBN: 0-7434-9041-X

First Pocket Books trade paperback edition February 2005

10 9 8 7 6 5 4 3 2 1

POCKET and colophon are registered trademarks of
Simon & Schuster, Inc.

Designed by Richard Oriolo

Visit us on the World Wide Web
http://www.simonsays.com
http://www.wwe.com

Manufactured in the United States of America

For information regarding special discounts for bulk purchases,
please contact Simon & Schuster Special Sales at 1-800-456-6798 or
business@simonandschuster.com

Contents

Taking a steel chair to the head is sometimes the easiest part of the day for your favorite WWE Superstar. ✦ You would expect that wrestling for the fans is the most rewarding thing a Superstar can do, but easiest? Consider that, for the few hours leading up to the time you watched them strut to the ring, each Superstar had to get to your hometown from wherever they may have been. Maybe they just flew in that morning from another time zone and spent most of the flight restraining a drunk passenger who was punching people for no reason. Or maybe they stayed at a hotel four hundred miles away that didn't put too much of a premium on cleanliness.

These stories are all part of what happens to the WWE Superstars when you're not watching them. When they're busy going from town to town to do the one thing they love more than anything—entertain the fans. It's the only job most of them ever wanted.

It's a job that keeps them on the road for over 240 days each year, but lets them see parts of the world many never dreamed they'd visit. It separates them from their families for incredible stretches of time, but introduces them to their "other" family.

It's a job unlike any other.

Their time traveling the world has given them incredible memories and lasting friendships. From the early days trying to make a name in the business to the night they first won the World Heavyweight Championship, many of your favorite WWE Superstars now share their most personal experiences from life on the road.

Are We There Yet?

One

The Good . . .

"I guess what's fun for some is just an animal sticking its head in your car for others."
—MOLLY HOLLY

WWE Superstars are constantly traveling the world but are never on vacation. Some have flown to Ireland for one day, and when they came back could only tell their families how nice the airport and arena were. The pubs? "Didn't have time." Others have been on four-day tours through South Africa. When asked about the beauty of the countryside, they'll tell you, "It looked great from inside the bus." ✪ But all Superstars will let you know that not every trip can go like this. You have to try and steal some time in between towns to do things you enjoy, to take your mind off the monotony of the traveling. As Molly Holly points out above, each person has a unique view on what is "fun," and that's what makes these stories so entertaining.

Perhaps the greatest of them all are the stories that didn't involve any planning. Through some odd coincidence or series of events, the Superstar was taken on a journey he never expected and will never forget. One saw his WWE career blossom thanks to a bus ride in England, while another discovered the most important thing in his life during a road trip to a Pay-Per-View in Pennsylvania.

From Cena to Superstar

John Cena

If not for one specific trip in Europe, I would still be searching for my connection with the fans. My chance to develop my free-stylin' character arose from something we were doing to pass the time during a bus ride in England.

We were on the *Rebellion Tour* in the fall of 2002, and that's one of the few times that everybody travels together. WWE chartered most of the trip for us. Our travel arrangements were covered for the two rides over the ocean, then for most of the trips in between the cities while we were over there. By the end of the week, the traveling got real long and tedious. In the span of seven days we went from Memphis, Tennessee, to Helsinki, Finland, to Belfast, Northern Ireland, to Manchester, England, to Sheffield, England, then to Grand Rapids, Michigan.

So we took the first charter flight to Finland. We did a show in Helsinki, then boarded another charter flight over to Ireland and one more to England. Now, the England shows were in two different towns that weren't far away from each other, so we took a bus between them. After the last show, we got back on the bus to head to the airport. It's quite a drive and we're all just kind of hanging out doing whatever. The tour's over, everyone is exhausted, but we're all wired with energy, you know that feeling, kind of punch drunk. I think it was because of the shows. Whenever we go overseas the fans are incredible, they are just awesome to us. All that energy in the building was keeping us going on the bus.

Now, we ended up having a lot of guys in the back of the bus who all like hip-hop, guys like Rikishi, Rey Mysterio, and Chuck Palumbo. We all just started rhyming. It got to be my turn and, man, I must have freestyled for like five or ten minutes straight. It was just flowin'. Little did I know that in the front of the bus was half of the creative team who heard it and said, "We gotta do something with this."

I'd freestyled backstage at *Raw* before, but just in front a few of the guys. On this bus was the first time a lot of people could hear, and it gave me a huge opportunity and pretty much launched my career.

Strip Steak

Mark Henry

I know every strip club in every city in America.

When we're out on the road I go to strip clubs in all the cities we travel to. You name a city—BAM!—I'll tell you the names of all the clubs there and what they're like. Atlanta, Georgia, has the best strip clubs in America. There is no debate as far as I'm concerned. Big, tall, thick, athletic women that are just beautiful. And man, I like beautiful women.

L.A. has some cool places, too. There're these three

clubs I go to there and they're the only places I visit when I'm in L.A.

I've been pretty much everywhere and, like I said, Atlanta is the best. You'll hear a lot of people say that the clubs in Florida and Texas are the best, but the places there are weird to me. They are more, well, you can say they are not exactly on the upscale side. I will admit that Florida and Texas do have a couple of good ones, just not better than Atlanta.

See, it's tough to compare them, because you can't put every strip club in the same category. I think you can break them down into two different types: gentlemen's clubs and go-go bars.

At gentlemen's clubs you have people in suits working the door and they'll seat you at a table and the place is also a nice restaurant. You can order a steak or lobster and have your choice of fine wines. All the while this is going on, you have beautiful women dancing around for you to admire while you eat and relax.

Then you got your go-go clubs. This is where girls dance up on the stage or on a bar and you throw dollars at them and drink alcohol. So many of these big go-go clubs that people say are real good, you won't see me in those clubs. They are like holes in the wall, and the standard of women, I hate to say this, but it's more low class. I'm not an overly classy person, but I can't go into these places where they let the women grind all over you. I can't take that. I'm a neat freak. If I see dirty chairs or dusty countertops I'm not going to sit there, forget about getting something to eat in a place like that. I'm nervous to go into those types of places because I don't know what's taken place on some of those seats before me.

I don't drink alcohol so I'm not a regular bar guy. I won't go to a bar just to stand around and drink all night. I don't go to these gentlemen's clubs to get drunk and disorderly, I go because after a show or a long drive, I want to eat dinner and see pretty girls. I don't see nothing wrong with that at all.

Someone once told me they thought it degrades women, but that's ridiculous. I'm admiring women at these gentlemen's clubs. A lot of time when I'm eating, I'll invite one of the women to sit with me at the table and I'll talk to them. Many times I've told them that they are beautiful and seem intelligent and should do something else with their lives.

Maybe I'm contradicting myself . . . that I like to go admire beautiful women at gentlemen's clubs but when I'm there a lot of the time I advise them to stop working there.

I don't know, I'm just a guy who likes to look at beautiful women when I relax after a long trip.

Where's Your Corncob Pipe?

Teddy Long

You want to talk about a crew? I was driving with APA [Ron Simmons and John "Bradshaw" Layfield] and Godfather this one time from Rochester to Albany, New York, in a snowstorm. I'm not talking little flakes here—it was really coming down. And we're on this road in the middle of nowhere, late at night; there is absolutely nothing around us, no other cars anywhere. Just nothing.

All of a sudden, Ron yells out from the back, "Hey,

Long! Pull over, I gotta take a leak." Now, I wouldn't have gone out in this weather, I don't care how bad I had to go. But if he wanted to get out there, I wasn't going to stop him.

When I pull the car over, everyone decided to get out and take a leak but me. I stayed in the car waiting for everyone to get back in. I took off right when I heard the doors shut. Bradshaw, who was in the passenger seat, looked over and asked, "What about Ron?"

"What about Ron?" Now I was just playing with Ron, I'm not serious with this. I thought he was in the backseat, so I'm waiting for him to say something back at me.

We're about half a mile down the road and Bradshaw asked again, "Long, what about Ron?" This time I turned around to say it to Ron's face and I see he's really not in the car. Bradshaw wasn't messing around.

So I had to back up on the interstate, in a blizzard, for half a mile to pick Ron up off the side of the road. When we got to him, he looked just like a snowman. He stood in the same spot the whole time, didn't move, just stared down the road at us because he couldn't believe I took off without him.

He was covered in snow from top to bottom. The Godfather opened the door for him and he just looks in and yells at me with that deep voice, "What the hell you doing, Long?"

We're all staring at him covered in snow, looking like Frosty, and just started laughing. For the rest of the ride into Albany, that's all he kept saying, "What the hell, Long?" Bradshaw, Godfather, and I didn't stop laughing about it for days.

Weirdo in the City

Shannon Moore

With this job, I've now seen so much of the world, whenever I go home, I'm always like, "God, this place is so boring. Nothing ever happens here. I gotta leave." But I know I'm never leaving my hometown. I could never live in a big city.

Like, I could never live in New York City, but I love to visit there. It's shocking to me; going to downtown New York City, a place that's always in the movies, you see it on TV all the time. And to be there and see it all in person is like culture shock for me.

One of things I love most about New York is that there are just so many different people there. With all my tattoos and piercings, everyone looks at me when I'm home like I'm a weirdo. That's me, the town weirdo. When I'm in New York City, I'm nothing but a regular country boy. I mean, you walk down any street and you see people with their faces tattooed and piercings the size of baseballs through their ears. Nothing's unusual there. You fit in no matter where you're from or what you look like.

I just like to walk around when I'm in New York. There's always something to see, something going on no matter what time it is.

When we go to some other towns and I'm looking for something to do, I always go to a mall. I don't know why I have this obsession with malls. I understand that all malls have basically the same stores—whether I go to a mall back home in North Carolina or one in L.A., it's pretty much the same thing—but for some reason I have to go every chance I get.

I've actually given the mall a lot of thought recently, and what I discovered is that I'm afraid there is going to be that one particular thing that'll be in a certain a mall and nowhere else. Like the Hot Topic in a Texas mall is going to sell this one T-shirt that the Hot Topic back home, in the Crabtree Mall in Raleigh, isn't going to have. Because of this job, I know pretty much every T-shirt that every Hot Topic sells throughout the country.

A Moment of Clarity

Matt Hardy

The night of September 17, 2003, was one of those nights when I knew I was starting to get sick. You know how those nights go. You have the chills one minute, then you're sweating to death. Your entire body aches. You know there's a fever coming on.

I thought I'd just go to bed early that night, sleep it off. Through the whole night, I woke up like every hour. My stomach was upset, I was drenched with sweat, I just felt brutal. When I got out of bed the next morning I had a terrible sore throat. It hurt every time I tried to swallow.

This was a Thursday morning and the only thing I could think about was that I had to be back out on the road Saturday, so I had two days to do what I needed to do to cure this.

I decided I would just go to the local drugstore for a

little NyQuil, maybe some cough drops or Alka-Seltzer. I didn't know that any of these things were specifically made for what was wrong with me, but I was thinking to myself that morning, "Hey, man, I'm Matt Hardy. I'm a tough guy. I'm a professional wrestler. I don't need to go to a doctor for this."

Throughout the day, I took the stuff I bought, but I wasn't feeling any better. My stomach was so upset it was to the point where I couldn't eat anything. I started having real bad diarrhea, too. It was official, I had a full-fledge case of sickness.

I got to bed early that night hoping one more night of rest might save me. It didn't.

When I got up the next morning my throat felt even worse. It was like murder. My whole body cringed every time I swallowed. There was no way I could eat, even though I was starving. I couldn't even drink water, it hurt so bad. Now this was Friday morning and I was heading back on the road the next day. You know, I hate going to doctors, but I knew I had to see one to find out what's going on with me.

He checked me out and said, "You should have been here two days ago. You have a severe case of strep throat. What we'll do is load you up with antibiotics, some throat medicine, and a special mouthwash. It'll relieve the pain in your throat."

As a WWE Superstar, there was only one thing on my mind. "Doc, I gotta ask you . . . I'm supposed to wrestle coming up this weekend. That's what I do for a job, I'm a wrestler. Will I be good to go by tomorrow?"

"For two days I recommend you don't do a thing except lay in bed. I would say wrestling is at least four days, maybe five, away."

I shook my head in agreement, thanked him, and walked out. I mean, I'm sure that was great advice he gave, but you're talking to a wrestler. We work through injuries and little sicknesses all the time. As I left the office I knew I'd be wrestling in less than twenty-four hours.

Saturday morning I woke up feeling miserable again, but there wasn't anything I could do now. Shannon [Moore] and I went to the airport and jumped on our flight to New York. We were booked in MSG [Madison Square Garden] that night.

Luckily, I was in tag matches all that weekend. I wouldn't have gotten through if I was in singles those days. Tag matches are obviously a little less taxing on you physically, but it was still brutal. This was definitely one of the worst states I've ever been in, as far as being on the road and being sick.

I couldn't even talk that whole day, I completely lost my voice. As we walked into the Garden, the fans were already lined up outside. They're screaming for you, all excited, and I knew I had to go in there and get through this, for their sake.

During the match I was able to do a couple spots, all my big stuff, then tag Shannon back in. He did the bulk of the match for us. And I battled through it. I felt worse than ever after the match, though. My stomach was so upset that I couldn't take it. I would have thrown up in the ring, but I hadn't eaten anything in a couple of days so there was nothing to come up. I was just dry heaving backstage all night.

We had to leave for Binghamton, New York, that night because we had an early-afternoon show the next day and wanted to get the travel over with. Shannon was great. He drove the whole time so I could sleep in the car, take my antibiotics, and just rest.

Our match in Binghamton was pretty much the same as the previous night. Shannon handled most of the work, I did a few spots and felt like death afterward. Then we got on our way for Bethlehem, Pennsylvania, which is where Monday night's show was. Around five P.M. we stopped along the way so Shannon could get a bite to eat. I tried to get some soup down, but it wasn't working. I passed the time by looking at the map to see the best way to get to Bethlehem. After I figured out our route I was just kind of looking around the Bethlehem area of the map when I noticed that Hershey was nearby.

It was at this point I realized that our show was early because the *Raw* folks had their Pay-Per-View that night in Hershey, and we wanted fans in the Binghamton area to be able to attend our show, then get home in time to watch the Pay-Per-View. I usually would have been all over this, but with being so sick and totally wrapped up in getting myself better, it just never hit me. I was out of it physically and mentally for a few days.

This information about the show times was important because I talked to Lita earlier in the day and found out that she was going to make her return at the Pay-Per-View that night. She had been out of action for fifteen months with an injury, and the whole thing sucked. It obviously sucked for her, but it was bad for us as a couple because it put us on different schedules for the first time in a long while.

We had traveled together for two and a half years before she was hurt. We both went through a pretty intense adjustment period when she first came off the road. It was a challenging time.

Toward the end of her injury, the two of us talked

about her return match a lot. How she would feel walking out there, how fans might react, just everything. We talked about how great it would be if I could be there to watch.

Looking at the map with all of this in mind, I figured that Bethlehem is a few hours from Binghamton and Hershey is an hour and half past that. I thought it was possible.

I looked at Shannon. "I talked to Amy [Lita] today and I know she's going to come out on the Pay-Per-View. I figure she'll come out like eight-thirty. Would you mind if we drove past Bethlehem and all the way to Hershey so I can show up as a surprise? I know I'm sick as hell, I feel like shit and really need to get some sleep, but I know she'd love it and it would mean the world to me." This was the most I had spoken in three days.

Shannon was like, "Yeah, sure man. Let's get out of here." So we left the restaurant right away and took off for Hershey.

About fifteen minutes later we hit some serious road construction. This was going to put us behind schedule. We moved two miles in the next twenty minutes. I went nuts, thinking how it's killing our time.

I will admit that I have road rage issues. Not all the time, but in traffic I just become a completely different person, so I can't take this anymore, sitting there, helpless. I asked Shannon if he would let me drive. I was so fired up now, all I had in my mind was that I was going to be there for that match and nothing was going to stop me. Shannon knows I'm very hardheaded so he pulled over to switch.

As soon as I took over, I started driving like a maniac. I pulled over to the side of the road and drove in the breakdown lane, whatever I needed to do to keep moving. I'm swerving around cars right and left, keeping an eye out for cops because if we get pulled over that would have really killed our time.

I got through the traffic as fast as I could and when I hit the open highway I'm going a hundred miles an hour. I look over at Shannon and he has a face like "I'm going to die in this car."

We hit a few other slow spots and I flipped out at every one. I was getting annoyed thinking that if I'm going through all this trouble, especially with being so sick, and I miss her appearance because of traffic . . . man, I would not be happy. I knew I was going to be physically ill when I got there for sure, but if I missed her I'd also be mentally ill.

We pulled up at Hershey Arena at 8:58 P.M. I'd done everything I could to get there by 8:30, like passing cars on double yellow lines of a two-lane highway, running up on the shoulder. I did anything I could. I wish I could actually apologize to some of the people I passed because I'm sure they were scared.

When we got out of the car, Shannon wanted to punch me, and rightfully so. I had been driving like an idiot and would have deserved it if he hit me. I jumped out of the car, ran right to the back. I stopped at the first monitor I saw. As soon as I looked at it the camera cut to the curtain and Lita's music started.

An amazing feeling came over me at that moment. She came out and I got to see her whole match.

When it was over I walked over to wait for her. Everyone congratulated her when she walked through. As she's hugging everyone, thanking them, she caught a glimpse of me and froze. She was confused to see me there.

She ran over and gave me a big hug. We just stood there hugging for the longest time. It was a wonderful feeling; it really confirmed for me how special our relationship is.

It was one of those things that lets you know that you are meant for someone. I refer to it now as my moment of clarity; I was destined to be there with her.

Think about it, someone must have been watching over me to make sure I got there in one piece and on time. So many things had to happen for that moment to turn out the way it did: the first few matches ran longer than expected; the fact that I barely had enough strength to walk the few days before but somehow I was able to drive like a lunatic for a few hours; even the traffic we hit that was eventually responsible for me walking in the moment her music started. It was amazing.

We spent the night together in Hershey. During her match she chipped her tooth and couldn't eat anything and I was still so sick I wasn't able to get any real food down yet. So we hung out in her hotel room and ate ice cream all night. It was perfect.

What Did Happen to Tuesday?

The Hurricane

One of the toughest tours I had was also one of the most fun.

We did a three-day run in Australia, doing shows in

Melbourne and Sydney. We went out every night we were there. And I don't mean for a little bit, we pretty much went out all night. We flew from Sydney after the last show straight to Vancouver, whatever that flight was, like eighteen, nineteen hours. I have some friends in Vancouver and I called them when we landed. They met me at the hotel and we went out all night. I mean, this was right after the plane ride. I just dropped my bags off in my room and went out.

I got to *Raw* the next day and I haven't slept in forever. Even though I was tired, I had a match with Christian that night that turned out to be a great one.

Monday after *Raw* I went out with my friends again and stayed out all night. I was able to sleep for a few hours on Tuesday because we had an off day, then I went back out on Tuesday night.

When we got back in Wednesday morning at eight A.M. I called the airline and explained to the woman that I had missed my original flight.

"Okay, sir, when was it?"

"Monday."

"Monday? Today is Wednesday, sir. What happened to Tuesday?"

"I can't remember."

What a great couple of days that was—at least from what I remember.

Who Needs Seven Years of School?

Dr. Tom Prichard

I was working through the Southern states at the time I picked up the name Dr. Tom Prichard. It wasn't really through anything I did, but something that someone else did and then it just happened to be a case of right time, right riding partners, right pair of pants.

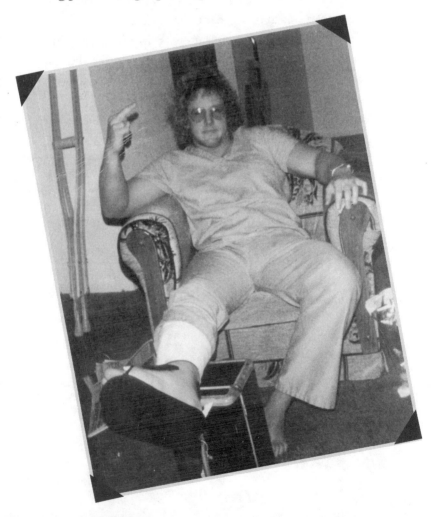

Robert Fuller and Jimmy Golden had been wrestling those Rich boys, Johnny and Tommy Rich, on this part of the tour. They'd been having some bloodbaths on TV, so Robert and Jimmy brought a cut man to the ring one night. You know, like the fight doctor for a boxer, and they put him in their corner. His name was Dr. Love.

At the end of the match, they knocked Tommy down and the cut man took out a roll of tape and taped Tommy's feet to the bottom rope. And they beat down Tommy and Johnny Rich. Robert and Jimmy double-teamed on Johnny while the cut man was taping Tommy down.

After a few minutes of that, they left the ring and went up to the interview stand where Gordon Solie was broadcasting to do a promo. "Hey, from now on we're not gonna have our pretty faces cut up anymore. From now on we're gonna have our official cut man with us, Dr. Love."

Now, we taped on Monday night and the show aired the following Saturday. The day after this show aired, Robert got a call from the FBI. They had been looking for good old Dr. Love, as there was a warrant out for his arrest. So Robert proceeded to tell them that Dr. Love just kind of stopped by that night and no one knew where he'd gone after the show or heard from him since. Needless to say, we never saw Dr. Love again.

We did a taping the day after we heard from the FBI and, of course, Robert and Jimmy had to go out there without their cut man. Once we finished up, Robert, Jimmy, and I were riding together to the next town and I'm lounged out in the back wearing these doctor pants that I got from Sherri Martel's roommate back in Nashville. I actually broke my ankle in Louisville during a match where me and Pat Rose, as the Heavenly Bodies, took on the Fabulous Ones, Stan Lane and Steve Keirn. Sherri was with our team, too, and we all drove together at the time. When we got to Nashville after the show, Sherri's roommate, who happened to be a nurse, gave me these doctor pants. With my ankle in as bad shape as it was, the doctor pants were the only thing I could get my leg in and out of without too much pain.

So I'm wearing the doctor pants, riding with the guys, talking about the Dr. Love thing and how they missed a great angle with it. That first night, the boys and Dr. Love got so much heat from the fans you knew it would have developed into something great. Robert was getting real pissed off over the whole thing and wanted to stop to get something to eat at the store and take his mind off it. As we're walking up, Robert caught a glimpse of what I was wearing, looked up at me, and said, "Damn, boy, you'll be our new doctor! Dr. Tom Prichard."

And that's how I got the name. Because this boy they brought out was wanted by the FBI and I happened to be riding with Robert and Jimmy the next week wearing doctor pants. I was put in the role and have been known as Dr. Tom Prichard ever since.

Would You Like to Drive?

Molly Holly

I'm not the kind of person to go from my hotel to the gym to the building and back again. I always try to see a little bit of wherever we are, especially on days when we have a house show and can get to the building a little later than usual. I never know when I'll be able to get back to some of these places, so I want to take advantage of it while I can. If there's a tourist attraction, no matter how cheesy, I'm there.

I was once driving alone from Lincoln to Omaha, Nebraska. Somewhere between the two I passed a sign for Wildlife Safari. I looked at the landscape around me and there wasn't much going on out there, mostly flat and dry, just like you'd expect the Midwest to be. I was curious to see exactly what the Nebraska locals classified as a safari.

A guy met me out front when I pulled into the parking lot. He explained to me that the safari costs five dollars a car and you had to stay under five miles an hour. This wasn't a ride that you got out to get on, you rode in your own car along a dirt path and passed a bunch of wild animals.

I figured five miles an hour didn't literally mean five miles an hour, but was more of a reminder to keep it slow. Well, I had no choice but to keep it under five because the roads were so bumpy. I've been on dirt roads before, but this was incredible. I'm going over huge rocks, then dropping down into ditches. The car is bouncing all over the place. My head was smashing up into the ceiling and I didn't even see any animals for a while.

I was all set to turn back around but figured I'd just drive it out and be on my way. I'm so glad I did; it turned out to be awesome.

There were humongous buffalo and these egret birds that were just so graceful and peaceful to watch. Then there was this great, big deer, it was absolutely beautiful, standing only like ten feet from my car. I stopped to take a picture and rolled my windows down.

The deer started walking toward my car. This particu-

lar type of deer is called a pronghorn deer and has two sharp horns that come out of its head. And it's coming toward me. It didn't look angry or anything, but I was still scared. I didn't know what to do so I sat there, perfectly still. It walked all the way over and stuck its head right in my car window.

I retreat all the way over to the passenger side, practically squishing myself up on the window. I slowly grabbed my camera, took its picture while its head was in my car, and then start telling him, "Go, go! Get out of here."

He didn't listen at first, but eventually took his head out of the window and went back to chewing on his grass. The second his head was out, I took off.

As I'm driving along, bouncing up and down, I was so excited. I started calling all the other girls to tell them what just happened to me. Under normal conditions, talking on a cell phone while driving isn't easy. On these roads, I was all over the place.

I started screaming to them on the phone, "You guys gotta come out to the Wildlife Safari! I'm not sure where it is, but it's somewhere between Lincoln and Omaha! The animals are unbelievable. I just had a deer stick his head in my car! Right in my car!"

And they were like, "Yeah, we're just gonna watch some TV here in the hotel. We'll see you in a bit."

"No! How can you waste your life away watching TV inside a hotel room while I've got deer jumping into my car?"

I guess what's fun for some is just an animal sticking its head in your car for others.

Some of the Best

Dave Hebner

I think about how lucky we all are to have this job where we get to travel all over the world. Places that people dream about visiting for a vacation, we get to see it all thanks to this wonderful job. It's challenging, sure, but there's a great side to it as well, and it's not something I forget.

There are a lot of places I like to visit when we're going around the U.S. I like the atmosphere in Los Angeles. I could never live there, but it's a great place to visit for a few days. And San Antonio. It's as laid back as laid back can be. I can't imagine a place that makes better Mexican food than some of the places in San Antonio. I feel like all I do is eat the whole time I'm there.

But no question, New York and Chicago are the places I most love to go. When I was growing up, I thought I'd never get to New York in my life. How many people today would like to go to New York just to see where the Twin Towers were?

Here's a guy like me who gets to go there two or three times a month to work. I have the opportunity to walk every street in New York City. When I'm there, I go all over the place. I know people save up for years, all their pennies, nickels, just to go to New York City once in their life, and I get to go all the time. That's not even to mention the fact that I work inside Madison Square Garden when I'm there. It's the most famous sports arena in the world. You know millions of people have seen MSG on television and think, "Boy, I'd like to go see an event there." And I have this job that lets me walk all around the place.

Now the thing about Chicago is that when it comes to talking about just work, going out there and entertaining our fans, nothing beats Chicago. It doesn't matter what building we go to in that city. Since I've been with the company, I think we've been sold out at every show. From the opening bell until Tony Chimel or Howard Finkel thank them and tell them it's time to go home, our fans don't stop cheering and yelling. It's an amazing atmosphere in that city.

I'll tell you how excited Chicago gets me. In the beginning of the summer of 2003, I scheduled a few days off for the end of September. Well, the live events schedule came out about a month before I was set to have the time off, and I noticed that during those days we were doing a run through Peoria, Chicago, and Milwaukee. I went right to

Johnny Laurinaitis, VP of Talent Relations, and told him "Hey man, you gotta put me back on. That's my town. I gotta work Chicago." I gave up my days off just like that.

I'm telling you, nothing beats Chicago.

R . . . R . . . R . . . *Rico Suave*

Rico

I travel with the Divas most of the time. It's especially funny because of my character. There are times when I get out of the car at a building, and a fan will yell something like, "Hey Rico! You're a queer!"

Then they see Gail, Ivory, Victoria, Trish, Miss Jackie—basically five of the most beautiful women they've ever met in person—following me out of the car, and I just give them a playful, wise-guy look and say something like, "Yeah, and it's real tough being me." They always get this face where their mouths open and their eyes drop in disbelief. It's great.

Even though a scene like that provides me with endless amusement, it's not the reason I ride with the Divas. And I don't ride with them because I like hanging out with beautiful women. I'm as married as married can be and have the most beautiful woman in the world at home.

I ride with the Divas because they are so easy to get along with. Most people have this vision of famous, gorgeous women . . . that they're difficult and high maintenance, but not our Divas.

I found this out one night on a drive from Maine to Prince Edward Island. Because we flew into New England and were going to fly out of Canada, there was a $250 International drop fee with the car rental place. To save some money, I jumped in with Ivory and Gail Kim along the way.

They had this big Lincoln Navigator. About an hour into our drive, we had a mechanical failure. We had no interior lights and because this was a brand-new model, everything in the car was digital. We couldn't see how fast we were going, how much gas we had, nothing like that. Gail drives pedal to the floor the whole way, so maybe it was better we didn't know how fast we were moving. These roads were all small ones, connecting Maine and Canada, and had no lights on them. So except for when the occasional car passed us in the other direction, we couldn't even see each other.

During the drive, we talked about staying at one of the nice beachfront bed and breakfast's on Prince Edward Island as a way to make up for this stressful drive.

When we got there, of course, they're all sold out. We ended up staying at some regular motel nowhere near the beach.

And they were both so cool with it. I thought, man, if these women can take this in stride, I mean the whole trip was miserable, then they would be cool to drive with all the time. So I started riding with them after that and the "Rico, you're a queer" joke came along as a nice bonus.

two

The Bad . . .

"So now we're on the wrong side of a major highway, going about ninety . . ."

—SHANNON MOORE

We've all been on trips that, for one reason or another, didn't work out exactly as planned. A flight delayed a few hours, a lost rental car reservation, or a hotel that wasn't quite as nice as its website promised. All of these minor inconveniences are annoying and likely to set you up for a bad few days. ❂ Unfortunately, WWE Superstars are forced to overcome these kinds of obstacles on a regular basis. Sure, there are times when the situation is a bit extreme, and they're forced to use their T-shirt as a pillowcase and sleep fully clothed to avoid any direct contact with the bed linens, but for the most part, they're resilient by now.

Near-death experiences, promoters making them drive 2,500 miles in a weekend hoping it would make them quit, and of course, run-ins with the police. What many Superstars consider to be a truly bad trip would be a life-altering event for the average person.

Quit playing games (with Your Car)

Shannon Moore

A couple of years ago when we were working in Nashville, me, Joey Matthews, Christian York, and Hurricane wrestled as a group called the Badstreet Boys. It was a boy band gimmick. When it started to take off a bit, we were set to shoot a music video as part of the angle.

Now, we all lived in the Carolina area, so we had to make the nine-hour drive to Nashville all the time. It just became routine for us. We're all excited for this particular trip though, the one where we were going to do the video at TV's, because it was our first big thing with this band and we really thought it was about to take off.

We all met at Joey's house in Hickory, North Carolina, that day. He was driving this time; we always rotated who drove. Somehow Joey convinced his sister to let him take her new Honda Accord on this trip.

There we are cruising on 40 West, which would take us right into Nashville, talking about our ideas for the video and the development of the angle after that. We were going for a while and then me and Hurricane fell asleep in the back. Then Christian fell asleep in the passenger seat and before you know it, Joey falls asleep with the cruise control set at eighty.

The car is now speeding down 40 West with the driver fast asleep. *Crash!* My body was thrown around the backseat. We slammed into the back of another car. When I opened my eyes, we're spinning around. The car smashed through the median and ended up in the oncoming traffic.

Joey is absolutely freaking out. Because he's panicked, he's stomping on the gas instead of the brake and not even realizing it. So now we're on the wrong side of a major highway, going about ninety. Christian reached over to grab the steering wheel and pull the car back into the median, out of the traffic. Everyone in our car was okay.

Hurricane now takes off running toward the other car. When he gets there he sees it's a woman and she's not moving, she's in total shock. We wrecked both cars so bad. The woman was fine, but she didn't want any part of talking to us.

Obviously the cops came, it was a huge deal. We found a place nearby that could fix the car up enough to get it to run. They had to bend stuff, put new tires on, all sorts of things. We made it to Nashville a few hours later and had to go right to the building. You must have been able to tell that we'd had a rough trip, because when we got there, everyone said we looked like crap. They gave us the day off and told us we needed to go get some rest. We shot the video the next day.

For the rest of our time making that drive to Nashville, we played Pearl Jam's "I'm Still Alive" when we got on Interstate 40. And Joey's sister never let him borrow her car again.

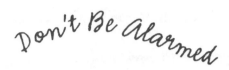
Don't Be Alarmed

Brooklyn Brawler

When Giant Silva was around, Harvey Whippleman and I would have to babysit him because he didn't speak English. We thought that since we were stuck lugging this humongous guy around with us everywhere we went, we might as well benefit some. So we would make him drive us around on long rides.

We'd get these vans, rip out the middle seat, and sit in the back with a cooler of beer while the Giant drove. So one night we're driving through California and all of a sudden we see cop lights behind us.

"Uh, oh, Giant, it's the cops. Pull over."

"No."

He said this and kept on driving as if there's nothing going on at all. Running from the cops is not something I want to mess around with, so I'm in no mood for games.

"Pull the car over, Giant, it's the cops!"

"I do nothing, so I no stop."

Now this cop must have called for backup right away because now we have a second car chasing us.

"Giant, I'm not kidding. You pull this damn car over right now!"

I'm screaming about as loud as I can and Giant's not even flinching. He's as calm as ever. "I don't know why they look at me, I do nothing. I no stop."

I gave it one more try. "Pull the damn car over right

now!" For some reason he listened to me this time and pulled onto the shoulder.

As the cop is walking toward our car, I jumped up from the back to stick my head out the driver's side window and yell out, "Officer, please do not panic, but he's a giant!" The officer was so startled that he just stopped walking and looked at me all nervous.

"Is he a violent giant?"

"Not usually, but he's very large and might get scared."

They continue to make their way toward us and instruct Giant to get out of the car on his own. As soon as they have him out they want to do a drunk test. The problem was, they couldn't see in his eyes. Standing in front of Giant they were like face to upper stomach.

To get eye to eye they made him get down on his knees on the side of the highway. Once he's down there they start shining a bright light in his face.

I looked over at Harvey and said, "What if someone from the office drives by right now? Can you imagine what Vince would think if he sees Giant Silva on his knees on the side of the road with two cops shining a flashlight in his face?"

At the time we were worried, but looking back on it, being spotted wouldn't have been all that bad. If the office had seen it, they probably would have gotten nervous about Harvey and I babysitting Giant and not want us to do it anymore. I wish we'd thought about that back then, we would have confessed the incident right away.

The Last Ride?

Victoria

There were a bunch of us in the Atlanta airport, all traveling home to different places after a weekend of live events. One of the conversations we had while we were sitting around the gate ready to go our separate ways was about hitting animals when driving. Al Snow joked about how he has the worst luck of anyone, and although it's always an accident, he thinks animals are magnetically drawn to the car he's driving.

The plane to Louisville was ready to board, so Rob Conway, Rene Dupree, and I all got on. Rob was in front of me, Rene was a few rows up. We're cruising along and all of a sudden there was a loud *Boom!*

Immediately, the plane dipped so far to the right that I thought we were going to roll over. Everyone was silent . . . everyone, that is, except me.

I started screaming, "Omigosh! Should we call our families?" Rob stayed real calm even though I was yelling right behind him, he reached back and grabbed my hand. Rene turned around and gave this solemn stare.

The captain broke the silence and came on the loudspeaker to say that a bird flew into the engine. We had to return to Atlanta.

Right away, I yelled out, "No way! I don't think birds fly this high!" In retrospect, I wasn't helping the situation at all, just freaking out everyone who could hear me. Then I felt the plane descending way to quick. I didn't know what was going on.

Apparently, when the engine went out, and the plane leaned on its side, we had turned around to change direction back to Atlanta. I didn't know that. So as we were descending, I'm screaming, "Oh my God! They're looking for somewhere to put the plane down! An emergency landing!"

I wanted to call my family, but I didn't want to disrupt what I thought was the pilot's attempt to safely crash-land this jumbo jet. In my mind I was getting ready to die.

It was the first and only time in my life that I ever went through that. I remember thinking that I was proud of the life I had led, and that I would be reunited with my grandparents in Heaven. I really made peace with the whole process.

But I didn't need to. We landed safely back at the Atlanta airport in no time.

There were so many fire trucks and emergency crews on the runway, it seemed like a much bigger deal than it turned out to be. I got off the plane and called my family crying.

When I hung up with them, the first thought I had was, "I'm never flying again!" Well, it only took me a couple of hours to relax back in the airport before I was on another plane for Louisville. I'll take a million more plane trips in my life, but this is one that I will never forget.

This Room . . . Is not So Sweet

Molly Holly

I was the Women's Champion in the early days of the brand extension when the champions would work on both shows. I wasn't always sure if I'd work on *SmackDown!*

though. They only had a couple of girls on that show, so I wasn't going to defend my title every week. If there were plans for me to be on, they usually told me a couple days beforehand so I could make arrangements. I always like to have all my reservations made before every trip. It's how I spend my off day—planning the next trip.

One night at the end of a *Raw* taping in Philadelphia, an agent came over to me and said that plans had changed for Tuesday's show; they needed me to be in Wilkes-Barre, Pennsylvania, for *SmackDown!*

I called the airline right away to change my departure airport to something closer to Wilkes-Barre and postpone my flight home by a day. Then I was going to call a hotel in Wilkes-Barre to book a room for the night but decided I'd wait until I got there to do it in person. I needed a room for one night in Wilkes-Barre, Pennsylvania; I didn't think it would be big deal.

I drove around to the usual hotels after Tuesday's show—Hampton Inn, Marriott—and they were both sold out. I figured no big deal, that happens sometimes. I'll just check out a few more. Holiday Inn, booked. Days Inn, booked. Red Roof Inn, booked. They're all sold out.

How could this be possible? I thought someone was playing a joke on me. In the fifth hotel I went to, I asked the clerk what could possibly be going on in Wilkes-Barre on a Tuesday night to cause this backup.

"Nothing special. Just the usual I guess." The usual? This is the usual amount of people Wilkes-Barre brings in on a nightly basis? I severely underestimated the drawing power of Wilkes-Barre, I guess.

What actually bothered me more than these five places

being sold out was that at each and every one of them the front-desk clerks all said, "You should have made a reservation" before I walked out. They were kind of rubbing it in my face that I didn't expect them to be so busy. That wasn't the support I needed.

At around 1 A.M. I still hadn't found a hotel and started to get desperate. It was too cold to sleep in the car, and I wasn't about to drive too far out of the city because my flight was at six the next morning. I didn't want to have to get back up at 3 A.M. to get to the airport on time.

My window of opportunity to get any meaningful sleep was slowly closing. I decided to drive toward the airport, thinking the closer I was to it, the longer I could sleep in.

I went into the first motel I saw. They said they had one room left—the honeymoon suite. They have a honeymoon suite at an airport motel in Wilkes-Barre? As disturbed as I was by the existence of this room, I took it.

Inside the room was a huge hot tub, about two feet away from the bed, and there were mirrors all over the ceiling. I was pretty grossed out.

I took one of my T-shirts out of my luggage and used it for a pillowcase. I slept in full clothes and was still too bothered to sleep. The whole night I laid there trying to figure out what kind of people spend their honeymoon at an airport motel in Wilkes-Barre and was horrified to think about the types of things that went on in there.

The whole decoration of the room was seedy: It was all real dark—the walls, the carpet, everything was a dark color. It was all very sketchy.

Sorry, Wrong Room

Kane

When you're sitting around the arena all day, some nights you just can't wait to get out of there when you're done. At one show, I was in the last match but knew that after the bell there was going to be a run-in on my opponent by the guy he was feuding with at the time. They were set to go at it for a few minutes after I left the ring. I knew I wanted to beat the fans out of the arena so I wouldn't sit in traffic for an hour; these few minutes were my only hope.

I ran back to the locker room and didn't shower or anything. I just threw on my workout stuff from that afternoon—shorts, a tank top, sneakers. I didn't even put on socks. As I'm sprinting to the car, I realize I still had my makeup on, too. I didn't care. The only thing on my mind was getting out of that arena parking lot and to the hotel immediately.

The weird looks started the second I entered the lobby. I'm dripping with sweat, wearing wrinkled workout clothes, and had half my long hair pulled back in a ponytail, half hanging in my face. Between my hair and the eyeliner I was still wearing, I basically looked like the world's largest transvestite.

I checked in, walked up to the room, ripped open the door, threw my bag in and then noticed an old couple sitting on the bed. I had no idea where they came from, they started screaming at me in some foreign language I couldn't understand.

I just . . . I mean . . . I had already put in a real long day, so I just sort of stared at them, cussing under my breath. Not at them. But at the situation.

They're screaming, just terrified. They both jumped up on the bed and were now like hugging each other as if they were saying good-bye or something. By the time I got back down to the front desk, the clerk was already on the phone with this couple apologizing, telling them he was going to give them a free lunch and stuff.

I think they saw their life flash in front of their eyes at that moment, and I can't say I blame them.

Think about it, if you can imagine a seven-foot, three-hundred-pound guy, wearing mascara, slamming your door open . . . that's a pretty scary sight.

Driving Me Out of the Business

Jim "J.R." Ross

A rough road trip once led me to quit the business for a couple of years.

There was a power change at the top of the Oklahoma

Another Monday night, setting up for another *Raw*.

territory. Cowboy Bill Watts, who was the head booker of the territory, had a falling out with the new man in charge and went back to Atlanta to book and write TV for TBS rather than stay and deal with the bull. This was in the glory days of TBS, so it was a good move for Cowboy.

He wanted me to go along with him, but I was newly married at the time and knew my going to Atlanta wasn't going to work out for me and my wife. Although Watts was my ally, me and the new guy in charge got along very well. But that didn't matter much.

Just like in Washington when there's a regime change, when the Democrats take over the presidency or the Republicans take over, whenever there's a change at the top, it sets up a series of changes regardless of who you are or how well liked, or not liked, you are by anyone.

The deal was, though, instead of just coming up to me and saying they wanted to make a change, it was decided they would make me quit. I was refereeing at this time and they knew my heart was not fully into that aspect and that I wanted to do other things in the business. They could have used that as a reason to get rid of me, but no, they decided to literally drive me out of there.

Making referee money, which back then was like $40 a night, they knew I couldn't afford to fly anywhere, I had to drive. They booked me on a tour that had me working in New Orleans, Louisiana, on Thursday; Oklahoma City, Oklahoma, on Friday; Monroe, Louisiana, on Saturday; and finish up on Sunday in Joplin, Missouri.

From a mileage standpoint it was about 725 miles from New Orleans to Oklahoma City, then 500 the next night, and 475 on Saturday night. Oh, and don't forget the 800 miles I had to drive to get to New Orleans from where I was living in Oklahoma at the time.

So they booked me on a four-day, 2,500-mile tour.

It was immediately obvious to me that I was given this trip as part of wrestling politics. The usual run would have been working either the south end, Louisiana and Mississippi, or the north end, Oklahoma City, Tulsa, Springfield, the whole time. Someone was sending me a message with that booking. It was my first taste of wrestling politics.

Even though I knew what was going on as soon as I received the assignment, I wasn't going to go to the boss and tell him I wasn't doing it. I didn't want to burn a bridge or anything like that and be put out of the business forever. This trip alone didn't beat me; I had already been thinking about taking a break from the business before anything happened with this trip. It was the thing that pushed me over the edge though.

It was clear to me that this kind of stuff was going to continue. I'd be forced to drive 2,500 miles every week. I wasn't a very good politician, no matter what people might say, and wanted no part of it. I resigned.

I had other business opportunities and with the encouragement of my then wife, I bought a department store in my town and got out of the business full-time for seven years. I knew I didn't want to get out of the business forever, but I needed to step away for a bit for my own good. I had started some bad habits just to stay awake, things like smoking and drinking more black coffee than should be allowed. If I continued the way they were going to make me, 2,500 miles a week, I know these habits would have only gotten worse.

I Think You're Actually Looking for a St. Bernard

Teddy Long

I was driving with the APA one time, going from Lexington to Louisville, Kentucky. Bradshaw was in the front, Ron was in the back, and I was driving. Now these two had been drinking beer all night long; they were totally drunk.

There was some construction at one point that blocked some of the road and I missed the exit we needed. I didn't think it was a big deal, I'd just have to get off at the next exit and turn back around. Well, I ended up having to go like seventy miles before there was another one. I couldn't believe it. Seventy miles. By going this far out of the way I had to make up time by driving quickly.

And wouldn't you know it, I get stopped by the cops. So the cop is talking to me and I have John in the front, he's drunk, and Ron in the back, and he's drunk. Ron started kicking the seat, screaming, "What they want from us, Long? What they looking for, Long?"

I asked Ron to stop kicking my seat, but he's not listening. Now I'm trying my best to ignore Ron and talk to the police, but finally, the police leans in the car and said, "I smell alcohol in here." And he was right. I didn't have a drop to drink all night, but these two in the car were dead drunk. They weren't driving, so it's not like we did anything wrong. We'd be okay.

Then out of the blue, Ron yells from the backseat, "Oh, you a bloodhound now?" He says this to the police!

Not wanting to make this situation any worse, I won't even turn around and look at him. Maybe if I ignored him, the cop would, too. Well, he didn't. The cop glared back there and warned him, "Sir, you need to be quiet."

Now the police is understandably annoyed that Ron is mouthing off, so they pull me out of the car to give me the sobriety test. They gave the walk the line, the A, B, C gimmick, the count to sixty—all that stuff. The guy sees I'm not drunk so he lets me off with a little speeding ticket.

I knew he had to give me something for all that Ron put him through, but he didn't lay anything too major on us.

Just a Little Rail Sliding

Matt Hardy

I wasn't twenty-five years old when Jeff and I first got into the WWE, and in a lot of places you have to be twenty-five to rent a car. The office would usually take care of it for us, but sometimes, once we got to the town, we'd have trouble picking it up because of our age. We'd usually grab a ride with the Headbangers when that happened.

The four of us were riding together one time from Chicago to Milwaukee. I was driving, one Headbanger was in the passenger seat and Jeff was in the back with the other one. As we were driving down the road, we ran up on Mark Henry, who was driving real fast, like ninety, so we settled in behind him. We're kicking it down the highway. Then we hit a spot right before Milwaukee that suddenly slowed down. It was actually more like stopping than slowing.

We were coming up over this hill and all we see are brake lights. There wasn't much warning at all. Mark slammed on his brakes. I slammed on mine but realized I didn't have enough time—I'm going to crash into Mark if I don't pull off the road.

But Mark had the same idea about the person in front of him, so just as I swerve, Mark did, too. I knew I was still gonna hit him unless I pulled up even farther on the side of the road.

Now we're going so fast that I couldn't just come to a complete stop. The car would have skidded, I would have rammed into Mark in front, and the person driving behind me was sure to whack us.

Right before we came over this hill we passed an exit. You know how, near some exits, they have those small metal retaining rails? The ones that start kind of angled up, like they're coming out of the ground, and get higher as they move along, so if a car would actually slide into it the rail would hold it on the road. Well, what happened was that because we had just passed an exit, I actually ended up pulling right on to one of those rails.

As the rail rose up, so did half of our car. I was driving on it, sort of like we were rail sliding, like we had invented a new extreme sport. We were only on two wheels for a while, so I didn't have too much control over the car and couldn't stop it.

One of the Headbangers started yelling, "Oh my God, we're gonna die!" Now Jeff, being the person he is, just reached up from the back, put his hand on my shoulder and as calm as can be said, "Hold it steady now, Matt."

Even with all the craziness going on around me, I thought it was great advice. So that's just what I did. I was trying to hold it as tight as I could until the rail dropped back down enough to where I could pull off it. I rode that rail for what felt like a mile, but it was more like 100, 150 feet when we got out and looked back at it.

The car still ran after the rail incident, but there was definitely something wrong with the gas tank. From that point on, we could only fill it up to like eight dollars. I think we dented that tank pretty good and the gas could only get in part of it.

When we got to the facility that day, Mark was the first person we ran into.

"Oh man, I thought you all was dead! When I saw you hit that thing, man, I thought it was all over for you guys."

"Dead? Nah, just a little rail sliding," I told him.

Later on that day, I wondered why, if he thought we were dead, he didn't stop to help us out or something. I should ask him that one day.

Sleep at Your Own Risk

Ivory

When I first started out I didn't feel like I should be asking for rides, like I had to prove that I could take care of my own business. Travel was one of the biggest things in this, so I was organized about it, planning my routes, making reservations way in advance, all of that.

During a big ten-day tour up the East Coast, we had to drive from New York to Rhode Island in one night. One of the other women had warned me about this night in advance. She told me the area we were heading to had nothing around it, and gave me the name of a hotel to call for a reservation, saying it was our best option.

A few days before the New York to Rhode Island drive,

I offered Jacqueline a ride during the tour. I had never driven with her before, but saw it as a great chance to spend some time with a veteran.

We made it to the town and found the hotel right away, and as we pulled up we couldn't help but notice that half of it is being renovated. The construction vehicles and scaffolding over most of the building tipped us off. Our room was in the part that was being torn apart, of course. Even without all the construction, this place was so gross and so scary and so Norman Bates-ish.

I'm low-maintenance, any place is usually fine for me. I'm not going to walk away because of a musty smell in the carpet or anything like that, and I'm telling you, this place was bad. Here I have Jacqueline, a respected veteran with me, and she's looking at me like, "You've got to be kidding me, rookie."

I started apologizing to her right away, telling her I had no idea, which was true. Believe it or not, the place was a brand-name hotel, one that I'd stayed at in other towns—I guess it's just hit and miss with that. This place was so bad that when Jacqueline went to bed she put one of her T-shirts over the pillow so her head wouldn't touch the pillowcase.

The only thing that saved my ass from me being talked about in the locker room was that Howard Finkel pulled up right behind us and got turned away because he didn't have a reservation. So at least we had a place to rest our eyes for a bit, he didn't have anywhere to go. We got up pretty early the next day and got right out of there. It wasn't a place you wanted to stay any longer than you had to.

After that trip I kind of had an idea why Jacqueline kicked me so hard in the ring.

Have I Got a Deal for You!

Brooklyn Brawler

I rode with the Iron Sheik for a two-week run one time. He offered me a deal the first day: If I rented the cars, he'd pay for the hotels.

I thought this was a pretty good deal, so I jumped on it. Splitting it up this way would cost me a lot less, so I wondered why Sheik would do it, but figured he had some sort of a deal with the hotels we were going to stay at and wouldn't be paying full price.

Yeah, he had a deal all right.

While we were checking into our hotel the first night, he told me he hurt his hand earlier in the match and couldn't write so I had to just sign the bill. He used his credit card. I was just signing. I saw him drop his card on the counter and saw them run it through the imprint machine, this was way before the scanners they have now. It all looked legit.

Little did I know he was using a fraudulent credit card at these hotels. Three weeks later the office called and told me they were given information that I was traveling around the country skipping hotel bills with a bad credit card. I actually had to go to the office to explain in person to everyone what happened in order to save my job.

They called the Sheik right after they got done with me, and he said he did it as a joke and was going to tell me the next time he saw me and pay the hotels once I knew about it. Because the hotels had called the office already, the office had to pay them right away to keep everyone out of trouble.

That was the last deal I ever made with the Iron Sheik.

We Should Have Upgraded to a Sled

Michael Cole

It was the winter of 2003, and a snowstorm—expected to be the worst in a decade—was bearing down on the Northeast. The brunt of the blizzard wasn't due until Monday, so Tazz, Josh Matthews, and I believed we could catch a flight out of La Guardia Airport on Sunday and be in Indianapolis in time for *SmackDown!*

Turns out, the forecasters were very wrong on when the storm would hit the New York area.

The 4 P.M. flight was delayed until 6 P.M., then 8 P.M., and finally 10 P.M. Before we could board the plane, the ticket agent had a few announcements to make. She told us that (1) the flight to Indianapolis would be the last one out before the airport shut down for an expected two days; (2) the airline would have to send all the bags on another flight after the storm because the pilot was concerned about carrying too much weight in the blizzard winds; (3) no children would be allowed on the flight.

That was all we had to hear. "This flight isn't going nowhere," Tazz said. "We're driving. We gotta get to *Smackdown!*"

We trudged through the snow to the Hertz garage and

rented a vehicle that the counterperson said was "equipped for snow." A few minutes later another worker pulled our car around—a Ford Taurus.

"You gotta be kidding me," Tazz said. "You want us to drive seven hundred miles through a blizzard . . . in a Taurus?"

"Well, it's front-wheel drive," the worker said. That wasn't going to cut it.

Four free tickets and a bunch of autographs later, we were in a Lincoln Navigator driving across snow-covered New Jersey. It took us five hours to cover the first eighty miles. After watching three tractor trailers jackknife and end up in ditches on I-78, we stopped in Allentown, Pennsylvania, for the night, hoping to get back on the road by 10 A.M. the next day.

The blizzard was even worse the next morning. Josh spent an hour digging the truck out from under two feet of snow. As we watched, Tazz asked, "You guys think we should wait it out a little longer?"

"The Weather Channel says it's letting up," I told him. "It looks like I-78 is cleared up now. It'll be over in no time." Famous last words.

Once we were out on the road, it didn't take long to see that the conditions were so much worse than the night before. There was no one else on the road! But that didn't stop Josh.

Hell-bent on driving the entire way, he navigated un-plowed roads doing seventy-five miles an hour. As Josh battled through fits of road rage and constant bouts of attention deficit disorder, I listened to hours of ECW stories from Tazz.

Apparently Tazz had wrestled in every town we drove through.

At ten o'clock Monday night—a full twenty-four hours after we left New York City—we pulled into Indianapolis ready for *SmackDown!*

And yes, Josh drove the entire way.

The End of a Challenging Era

Kane

Traveling has gotten a lot easier for me now that I don't have to wear the mask. When I was keeping my face covered, I would take extra measures to conceal my identity while I was on the road. I felt the mystery of it was a big part of the character's allure.

A lot of people would ask to take pictures with me when I walked from the arena to my car and I'd have to say no. I didn't like to have my picture taken. It was never because I meant to offend anybody or because I didn't want to be bothered. I was only trying to protect the integrity of my character as much as I could.

Most of the fans understood what was going on. I didn't want pictures of me all over the Internet. I knew it wouldn't be good for the character's development. I mean, it's inevitable it's going to happen, I'm not going to cover my face with a towel every minute I'm out in public, but I didn't want to make it easy for people to get. I didn't want to just hand it over.

Whenever it was possible, I would drive away from the building for a bit after a show before I got out to eat, think-

ing I'd have less a chance of running into the fans. I'd feel better about going into the restaurant with no cover this way. Fans would still come up to me and ask if I was a wrestler. I'd tell them I was but would never tell them which one. You'd be surprised at how few people were able to guess I was Kane. I always wondered why it was tough for them to figure out, it's not like we had too many guys my size out there.

There was this one group of guys who had been trying to take a picture with me for six years. They would ask me at every show they were at and every time I'd say no. They were the kind of guys who were cool about it, who understood.

I saw them in the Phoenix airport the morning after my first show there. I didn't have the mask on and went right over to them. I think I caught them off guard when I asked if they wanted to take the picture they had been after.

It was kind of cool; I had built a bit of a kinship with those guys over the years, and that day at the airport, the chase ended.

Welcome to the East Coast

Victoria

I'm a West Coast girl and I don't know how to drive in any sort of winter weather. The smallest bit of snow, sleet, whatever, I want no part of it. And lucky for me, during my first few months with the WWE, February shows in Huntington, West Virginia, and Columbus, Ohio, put us right in the middle of a heavy ice storm.

This storm had already started as most of us were flying into the Huntington area. I could see how horrible it was outside, so at the rental car counter I upgraded to a truck. Not that I have any idea how to use four-wheel drive or anything, but I figured going to the truck was a smart move because I knew that's what people do when it snows. I ran into Triple H and William Regal while I was at the counter and they offered to have me ride with them. I was still new at this point and wanted to show everyone that this rookie could handle a little rough weather, so I thanked them for the offer but assured them I was fine.

As I was walking out, I saw Molly Holly and asked her to ride with me—thank God I did. The weather was horrendous the entire way to the building. Because the driving was so slow, it took us much longer to get to the building than we had planned for. It took so much extra time that the two of us had to put our makeup and gear on in the truck. When we finally got there, we pretty much had to run right to the ring because we were up.

I remember when we were done I was happy with our performance. Fortunately, the two of us were comfortable in the ring with each other because we'd been working together for a while. We knew what we wanted to do in there and the agents we have helping us are simply amazing. All of those things together helped us go out there and give the fans a great experience, despite the fact that we had just gotten to the building and were still frazzled thanks to our ride through the storm.

When the match was over everyone was telling us we should get right on our way to Columbus. Now we never leave until the show is over because there's so much that can be learned watching the other Superstars perform. But with the weather outside, leaving seemed like a great idea on this night.

One thing became clear as soon as we got outside: This storm wasn't showing any signs of slowing down. As we drove along the highway, we actually saw power lines snap and trees fall over. Watching these things go on around me was surreal, I've never seen the winter weather break trees apart right in front of me. This kind of stuff just doesn't happen where I'm from.

We weren't too far down the highway when we hit a police blockade. They had to close the roads thanks to the power being out all over the area. We were told to get off at the next exit, but were in luck because there was at least a motel there.

The lobby is real dim when we walk in, there were a few candles keeping it from being pitch dark. With what we could see, we could tell there was a woman behind the counter and a couple of seedy-looking guys just hanging out in the lounge area in the dark. They weren't doing anything. They were just sitting there in the dark. As we're talking to the clerk, checking in and all, I can tell these guys are like hawks, staring right at us.

Keep in mind, both Molly and I went right from the ring to the car with no stops. That means we were still wearing our gear, makeup, and everything from the show. Of course, dressed like that, these guys start asking us what we do for a living. There is no way I'm going to say anything to these guys, so I pretend like I don't hear them.

After asking a few times, this one guy gets frustrated and just yells to the clerk, "Hey lady, put them right by our room tonight." Great. This is the last thing we need with a storm outside. We're stranded in some small motel in the middle of nowhere, no one knows we're here and we got weird guys wanting to hang out with us. This is all shaping up for a perfect evening.

Now, I don't consider myself a prima donna, but there is one thing about me that the other girls make fun of me for. I'm a Hilton Honors member. I don't know what to say, I love the Hilton. I like to have someone there in the lobby to greet me. I like not having to walk back outside to get to my room. That always creeps me out.

To her credit, the clerk offered to walk us to our room with her flashlight after we're all checked in. With these guys watching us, though, I didn't want to go right to our room, so we ask if there are any places to eat nearby. The clerk tells us there is a strip mall not too far down the road.

Getting back in the car probably wasn't the best decision, but we needed food, candles, and, more important, didn't want to be anywhere near those guys in the lobby.

Molly's taking it real slow on the roads. The storm still hasn't let up at all. We're both a bit nervous being out on the road. Then we saw a Wal-Mart. I will openly admit Wal-Mart is my favorite store in the world. Seeing it there in the middle of this storm made me feel like I was Dorothy catching my first glimpse of the Emerald City. After we bought some of the things we needed to get through the night, we noticed a Chinese restaurant in the area, too. It was actually closed but they let us come in and eat.

We headed back to our motel, parked near our room, and find out that the guys from the lounge are our new next-door neighbors. Not wanting to just stroll right past these guys to let them know we're staying next door, Molly and I time it just right and run straight from the car into our room without them seeing us. Molly brought her DVD player, and as we're watching a movie we hear the guys say they were making a beer run. Yes, we could hear their conversation through the wall.

Once they all piled in their car and took off, I ran right to the front desk and asked for a room change. The woman behind the desk asked me if there was anything wrong with the room, so I told her I wasn't comfortable being next to that group of guys. She laughs me off and says, "Oh, those guys are harmless!"

Saying it with such confidence, I figured that meant

she knew the guys so I asked if they worked there. "No, I just met them tonight. They're going to get me some beer." Wonderful! Real nice criteria you have for judging people.

What a great place to be stranded.

She eventually switched our room to the other side of the motel. It was definitely kind of spooky getting settled in for the night even though the weird guys didn't bother us once we made the switch. We had no hot water and had to do everything by candlelight. Once we were able to get out of our makeup and gear, we watched some DVDs until we fell asleep. We got up early the next morning to get right back out on the road. The storm had stopped, making the roads a little bit better to drive on.

I didn't care that there was still some ice on the roads. Molly knew she could get us to the building if she took it slow and I couldn't wait to get away from that motel.

As we pulled out of the parking lot I was thinking about how great it was that I ran into Molly back at the car rental counter in the airport. Not only did she save me from having to drive in this East Coast storm, but as a relative newcomer, it was nice to have quality bonding time with another WWE Diva.

I had to get over the fun of our little "Diva Bonding Night" quickly, though. Jazz and I were facing Molly and Jacqueline in a tag match on *Raw* in few hours.

When we finally got to the building, we told everyone our story. At the end of it, a lot of the guys looked kind of disappointed.

One of them spoke up and explained why. "That's it? I mean, didn't you guys have to snuggle together in one bed to keep warm? Was there anything like that between the two of you? Touching of any kind?"

"No, there was no touching! So sorry to disappoint you all. Nice to see you're relieved we survived the night."

I guess boys will always be boys.

three

. . . And the Just Plain Bizarre

"Do you realize the idea of three WWE Divas lying in the same bed, watching a lesbian film is probably a fantasy for quite a few guys out there?"
—VICTORIA

It's inevitable that when you have hundreds of professional wrestlers on a never-ending journey around the world, strange stuff is bound to happen. Some of it so outlandish, even the Superstars who live through it recount their story with a hint of disbelief. ❂ There are times when they bring it on themselves, but plenty of others when an interesting character met along the way provides an incredible memory. And that memory is not always a good one.

My First Title Defense?

Bill Goldberg

I beat Triple H at *Unforgiven 2003* to win the World Heavyweight Championship for the first time. From what I remember we put on a great show. Some spots in the match are a bit hazy because I caught a knee in the head and was knocked out for a bit. A nice bump swelled up on me while I was backstage talking with Trip and some other boys after the match.

Once we got out of the arena, I needed to get something to eat. I knew we had a long drive that night from Hershey, Pennsylvania, where the Pay-Per-View was, to Washington, D.C., where we were taping *Raw*, so I wanted to get something before we hit the highway. I remembered that I saw a diner down the street from the building on the way in.

When we pulled up I could see a ton of fans in there through the window and I just didn't feel like going in. My head was swollen; I felt like shit; I didn't want to have to deal with anybody. I didn't want to go in, but my girlfriend talked me into it.

Most of the people in the diner this time of night were fans who were at the show. They noticed me before we even walked in the door, but were very considerate. They all waited until we were done eating to come over and ask for autographs and pose for pictures. Everyone in the restaurant gave me a standing ovation when we left. I thought it was so cool.

Before we got out of there I turned back and asked the

fans if they wanted to come over to the car to see the belt. I was really appreciative of the respect they showed both me and my girlfriend and wanted to thank them, I guess. They all took pictures holding the belt and stuff. I was feeling real good about the whole night so far despite the lump and the headache.

I called the hotel in D.C. from the car to upgrade my room to a suite and give my limo driver the room we originally had so he could just stay with us for the rest of the run. Like I said, I was in a good mood after the diner scene. The hotel guy I spoke to said I was all set.

We roll into the hotel a few hours later, about three in the morning, and when I go to check in the guy at the front desk starts giving me attitude right away. I only explained that I had called during our drive to upgrade and he just starts yelling at me.

"Who did you speak to? There is no one here but me and I have no record of an upgrade for you. You know, now that I look at it, I don't even have you booked for a regular room."

I questioned him how that's possible if I just spoke to someone else who told me I was all set and he snaps back at me to watch my tone. Now I was annoyed for sure, but wasn't yelling or anything yet. My girlfriend is asking me to calm down, not that I was hot, but she knew I was getting there. She knows me too well.

"Let me see what I can do," the guy tells me. Me and my girlfriend kind of walk away to the other side of the lobby to get away from the situation. After twenty minutes of him doing or saying nothing to us, I go back over there ready to take any space that has a bed. I was exhausted from the match, had a huge lump on my head, and I wanted to relax. I was done waiting for the suite.

"I really need to get to sleep, so just give me the regular room, please."

"With that attitude you'll get no room at all."

"That's great. Just give me a regular room and we'll be on our way."

He puts his head down, starts to punch some keys on the computer, then finally takes out a room key. As he's handing it over to me, I sort of whisper to my girlfriend, "This is ridiculous."

The guy hears me and pulls the key away like he's an eight-year-old playing a trick. "What did I tell you about your attitude?"

I'm still calm but now my voice starts to raise and I ask to see the manager.

"I'm the only one here, sorry." Now we are going back and forth and voices are picking up. I was calm and respectful, but my voice was loud.

With the two of us basically shouting at each other, a security guard who had just shown up on the other side of the lobby makes his way over. This guy knew who I was and was cool. He asked me to explain what was going on so I did. The clerk became enraged as I'm telling the story.

He starts blasting at me, "I don't care who you are! I don't care!" Then he tried to jump over the counter to come at me!

The security guard was standing behind him at this point, so he grabbed his waist, restraining him, before he could get over. The desk clerk was able to get his head forward, so we are face to face.

This guy wasn't letting up with the screaming.

Then he challenges me to a fight.

This guy was maybe five-foot-eight, 150 pounds, maybe, and he's challenging me to a fight. I look at him and ask, "Don't you see who you're talking to?"

Now, in no way did I mean it like "I'm Goldberg, a big star and you should treat me like one." I meant it like "Dude, I'm six-foot-four, 290 pounds. You're half my size and you want to fight me?" Anyway, he took it the wrong way and it made the guy even more crazed.

"I don't care who you are! You think you're so special! I don't care! Let's go outside and settle this thing!"

The guard is really having to hold this guy back now. He was small, but he sure had some fight in him. I told the guard I just wanted to get out of there immediately. The security guard could see that there was something going on with this guy, I don't know if he was drinking or what, but there was something up with him.

So the guard puts the guy in the back office and tells him he better not leave until he comes back to get him. The guard then had to call someone in the corporate office to make sure my reservation got canceled and my card wouldn't get charged. I went up the block to another hotel and they put me right in the suite.

My poor girlfriend brought champagne and stuff to celebrate my becoming the World Heavyweight Champion, but by the time we got to the next hotel I was so mad I just wanted to go to sleep. I had such a great night between winning the title and my positive experience with the fans in the diner, then for this little bastard to ruin it all pissed me off.

Dr. Tom Prichard

Back when I was working Smokey Mountain Wrestling, there was another guy there named Tracy Smothers who I just loved to annoy. Getting under his skin was so much fun for me. Even though I did go too far sometimes, I couldn't help myself.

He was rough in the ring and would hurt a lot of

Molly Holly poses inside the General Lee (from the *Dukes of Hazzard*) with Ben Jones who played Cooter, and it was only forty-five miles out of the way.

people. It was never intentional, he was just clumsy is all. So I felt that picking on him was suitable revenge.

After I'd been in the WWE for a little while, good old Tracy came up as well, working under the name Freddie Joe Floyd. Another thing to know about Tracy was that he'd suffered a lot of concussions in his day, so he was pretty much crazy from all the hits to the head.

I was traveling in a big group for a Thanksgiving show. It was me, Jimmy Del Rey, The Rock 'n' Roll Express, Ricky Morton, and Robert Gibson. Somehow we got on the topic of Tracy Smothers and I said to the group, "Tracy Smothers is an idiot and you can quote me on that."

Well, Ricky decided to do just that in the locker room the next day. We were all working this huge battle royal and when Tracy got in the ring he wanted to kill me. He truly wanted to hurt me. I somehow made it through the match and out of the building alive.

That night I was riding with Brian Lee, while Tracy was with The Rock 'n' Roll Express. Turns out, they actually left the building before we did. On the drive, we passed them on the side of the road, making a pit stop.

I told Brian to stop our car and pull over to them. Brian hesitated, figuring no good was going to come out of whatever I was about to do, but he eventually stopped.

I wanted to work things out with Tracy because I was about to start a program with him and didn't want to get in the ring with him if he was really going to take a shot and hurt me. So I walked up to him over on the side of the road and he took a swing at me. Not the type of swing that said "I want to knock your head off," but more like he just wanted me to know that he was pissed at me.

We started fighting a bit and then some cops drove by us. They pulled over to break it up and ask us what the hell was going on. We told the cops that everything was fine; we were just working on some wrestling moves that we were going to perform in the ring the next day.

They bought it and told us they'd let us go, but would not tolerate another episode like that in their county. As they made their way back to their cars, Tracy started talking junk to me about how I'm lucky the cops showed up, things like that. So I start jawing back at him. Before you know it, we erupt into another fight.

The cops had enough this time. They said they were going to start hauling people off to jail if we weren't all in our cars and on the road in ten seconds.

Nobody cared who was mad at whom, none of us wanted to spend the night in the big house, so Tracy and I apologized to each other and got right back in our cars.

Welcome Home, Victoria

Victoria

My grandfather was an actor in Japanese movies. So although she's not Japanese, my mother spent most of her childhood in Japan. That's actually how my parents met. My father was in the air force and was stationed in Japan where he met my mom. You could see that my mother's time in Japan influenced her a lot, as there were a lot of things she took from the culture. For example, when I was a child she sang me Japanese children's songs.

Whenever I saw Japanese photographers backstage at

our WWE shows, I'd tell them my family history, even singing a few of the songs I learned from my mother.

I was really excited about my first tour of Japan with WWE—it was my first time there, the place where my mother grew up. When we got off the plane in Tokyo, everyone was kind of loopy from the really long flight. And the fans mobbed us like no other place. It's like we were rock stars.

The freakiest part, though? All these fans were singing one of the children's songs to me! It was surreal. I guess the photographer passed along the story of how my mother would sing me certain Japanese songs and it was reported all over the media.

At the shows there were signs that said things like "Welcome Home, Victoria." At one of the press conferences, they asked me several questions, none of them about wrestling, but all about my family and my mom.

It was all such a moving experience and one of my most treasured trips ever.

plane Ride to Stardom

Booker T

I wrestled in an organization called the Western Wrestling Alumni for almost two years. During this time, I also had a regular job, working six days a week at a place called American Mini Storage in Houston, Texas. My one day off was Saturday. Friday night was when I'd go perform, so that gave me Saturday to come back home, relax, recoup, and get ready for the following week. Plus, I was raising my son, being a single parent, it was hard, but, you know, you do what you gotta do.

At that time I didn't have to travel as much. Each Friday night when we performed, we'd tape shows for one week. Those shows were broadcast on ESPN every day at three P.M. I was only making $125 bucks for those five shows every week, but I never really thought about the money at that point. The experience was worth it because of the television exposure.

So this one time, my brother and I went down to the Virgin Islands for the WWA and it turned out that we were big stars there because a lot of the islanders had seen us on ESPN. Everywhere we went people wanted autographs and asked to take pictures with us. It was bizarre. I had no idea.

Immediately after I got off the plane at home I had to go straight to work. It was such an eye-opening experience. One day I'm in the middle of paradise, having tons of fans trying to hang out with me, and the next I'm back at American Mini Storage by six A.M., sweeping out storage rooms, renting out trucks, busting my ass. That trip was a strange one.

Divas in the Green Masks

Victoria

In the summer and fall of 2003, Jackie Gayda, Gail Kim, and I were traveling together all the time. We got along real well and enjoyed each other's company, but one night we got a bit closer than any of us planned.

We got lost on our way from the arena to the hotel after the show and drove around for an extra hour. A great start to our trip.

In our little group, Jackie is responsible for booking the hotels. We split up the travel chores, hotel, car rental, directions, that kind of stuff, and the hotels are always her thing. Once we were inside, she stepped up to the desk first because she had the itinerary and everything she printed out. Jackie always books over the same Internet site so the routine is always the same.

The guy behind the desk tells her the computer is showing no record of a reservation for her. After trying her name a few more times, he still has nothing. He tried to check for me. Nothing. And Gail. Still nothing.

This guy was so nice and very helpful. He kept looking through some things on the computer and finally saw that we were booked at another location of this hotel chain—over five hours away.

Jackie called the website she booked the room with and after looking into what happened, they apologized to her. Something went screwy on their end causing the problem with our reservation. The apology was great, but it wasn't going to do us any good right there. Jackie explained to the guy behind the desk that the website was going to cancel our reservations at the other place and we would all just take rooms at this location.

"I'm real sorry, but I've got one room left and it's only got one bed. If you're okay with that, it's yours."

Three women. One bed. It wasn't going to be the greatest night of sleep any of us ever had, but faced with the alternative of driving three hundred miles when it was already so late and we had to catch an early-morning flight the next day, it would be good enough.

As soon as we stepped into the room and got a look at the one bed, I said to the other girls, "I think a glass of wine may help the situation." We all dropped our bags and zipped down to the lobby bar.

Walking in, we could see that there were only hotel employees sitting around drinking but didn't think much of it. I asked for a wine menu and the bartender told me they were shut down for the night. Thinking I could get some sympathy, I told him our story. He still wouldn't serve us. I then offered to pay him three times the price of each glass of wine. He refused it. This was hopeless.

Because we had to wake up early to get to the airport,

none of us wanted to waste time driving around this town looking for a place to get a glass of wine. We might not even find anything. It wasn't worth the hassle. We'd just go back up to the room.

Now the three of us have this thing we do where we hang out in someone's room before going to sleep: we give ourselves facials. It's quality girl bonding time. With us all in the same room, we decided to do the facials, relax in bed, and watch a movie.

I have to mention that the facials we always do require us to keep on this weird-looking green mask for a while.

So we're at the green mask phase, we all get into bed and start watching this movie; I can't even remember the name of it. It was about a call girl. At some point she gets involved with another woman and there's some steamy action involved.

The three of us just start laughing at the situation.

I looked at the girls and said, "Do you realize the idea of three WWE Divas lying in the same bed, watching a lesbian film is probably a fantasy for quite a few guys out there? And imagine if they could only see us now . . . all sexy in our green facial masks. I'm sure this is how they all dreamed it would be."

Capture the Flag

The Hurricane

I had a real crazy time one night in Mobile, Alabama, during the summer of 2003.

That night at the show, three independent workers

who I've known for a real long time had tryout matches—Joey Matthews, Mikael Yamaha, and Amber Holly. The four of us and Alexis Laree, who had just signed her WWE contract at the time, we all went out together that night. The five of us have worked together and been friends for so many years, it was like a reunion or something.

We started out grabbing a bite to eat at the local Hooters. People were coming up to me asking for autographs and stuff. At Hooters, you can take your picture with the girls for like five bucks, so the manager came over and started selling the pictures people were taking with me and was pocketing the money somehow. He threw some of the Hooters girls in every shot, so I think that's how he was pulling it off.

This one guy got mad over the whole thing and wanted to fight me. He was drunk and annoyed that we were getting attention from the girls and the other customers. He yelled at me, "I don't know who you are . . . blah, blah, blah." He wouldn't stop and was being real rude to everyone, so I had to slug the guy in the jaw.

Everybody in the Hooters was watching the whole thing and what a jerk he was being, so I slug him, he goes down. Some of the guys from the kitchen came out to pick him up and throw him out of the place. The manager felt real bad about the whole deal so he took care of our bill.

We all went out clubbing and stuff after that and did significant liver damage with alcohol consumption and all that good stuff. When we get back in the Marriott parking lot, we decided to climb the flagpole in front of the Marriott and take down the Marriott flag as a souvenir. It's huge, about as big as a king-size bedspread.

But we didn't just run and climb the pole, we wrestled for it. Joey and I had an impromptu flag match right there in the parking lot and the winner got to keep the flag. Joey still has it. I don't remember how he beat me; I was the most drunk of the group, though, so it couldn't have been too difficult to take me down.

The whole idea of the wrestling match started back at Hooters, I think. That guy who made me punch him put us all in the mood to wrestle, it just took a few hours and a couple of drinks to come out.

Will You Be Serving Crazy Pills on This Flight?

Rico

Being recognized as a WWE Superstar can sometimes put you in strange situations. This one morning, I was on the first flight out of Fayetteville, North Carolina. We had just finished up a run through the Carolinas and I was on my way home to Vegas, with a connecting flight through Cleveland.

There was so much fog that morning that we kept getting delayed. Take off was pushed back so far that I actually missed the first two connecting flights I was scheduled on. We landed in Cleveland about ten minutes before my third connection was set to leave. Because of all I'd gone through already that morning, missing the first two connections and all, Delta was nice enough to put me in first class from Cleveland to Las Vegas. It was great; I was stretched out in this huge seat in the last row where first class ends and coach begins. They served me this excellent breakfast and I fell asleep pretty quickly after finishing it.

Next thing I know someone is tapping my shoulder. I half open my eyes and see the stewardess standing over me, looking concerned.

"Are you awake, sir?"

"Kind of."

"Well, I need your help if you don't mind."

"What do you mean you need my help? Is everything okay."

"Ahh . . . not really. There's another passenger back there hitting some fellow passengers, so I'm going to tell him to stop, but I'd like you to be there when I do it."

"What? You're kidding me, right?"

"No. No I'm not."

I whipped around in my seat, but the curtain separating the two cabins was pulled shut so I couldn't see to the back of the plane. The stewardess walked in the direction of the curtain and I got up to stretch. I was in no real hurry or panic; I was convinced one of the other boys was on the plane and pulling a rib on me with this.

The moment she moved the curtain aside, I see this guy smack another passenger all the way in the back of the plane. She wasn't kidding. When I replay this scene in my head these days, it reminds of a movie. The kind of scene when the camera goes from a wide shot and zips into a tight shot on someone. I saw this guy whack somebody and I zeroed in on him. Nothing else on that plane mattered.

I took off and shoved the stewardess down one of the aisles without even realizing it. The puncher had his back to me, so I grabbed him from behind when I got to him. The first thing I couldn't understand was that he's smacking other passengers around, and no one is doing anything about it!

So I have a hold of him from behind and he starts to fight me, swinging his elbows, trying to kick, everything. I cracked him once in the head to startle him, grabbed him with one hand on the collar of his shirt and the other on his belt, and ran him all the way to the back to slam his head right into the food cart. I let go and he dropped to the floor.

I started yelling at him to get up. He began to cry. I had no idea what he's thinking right now, so I put my foot on his neck to keep him in place. I didn't want to take any chances. I went back to my old cop mode, wanting to make sure everyone was safe.

The head stewardess came back with the zip ties, those handcuffs that planes carry. She wanted to lock him up. Then this other guy comes back and says he's with some "Special Forces." Special Forces? I asked Special Forces where he's been until now.

I had him watch the guy for a minute while I talked to the stewardess. He's crying, sitting on the ground, snot and tears are running all over his face. Pain does some funny things to people. Just a minute ago he was all tough slapping people around, now he's crying like a baby.

I told the stewardess that it was her decision whether to put the cuffs on him, but I wanted her to realize that once she put them on there's no passing go, there's no collecting

$200 . . . he goes directly to jail when we land. You can't unarrest somebody. I wanted her to understand that.

Perhaps it's just my patient nature, but I suggested we give the guy a chance.

"Here's what we'll do. You can give the people in the last row my seat in first class, Special Forces's seat, and that jerk's seat. He'll sit in the center of me and Special Forces the rest of the way. We'll wait until everyone gets off the plane in Vegas and let him go on his way.

"But it's up to you. If you want to arrest him, I'll sit on top of him the rest of the trip and we'll wait for the air marshal to come get him once we land."

She wanted to talk to him before making a decision. Of course he starts crying and apologizing so she agrees to give him a break. We made all the seating changes and get settled in the last row. I lean over to him and whispered, "You just sit there and relax, buddy. You're catching a big break here. Keep quiet the rest of the way, don't say a word. We've only got thirty-five minutes left in this flight, you sit there quietly and we'll all forget this ever happened."

He listened . . . for a few minutes. Then he started undoing the seat belt. I knocked his hands away and told him to keep it on. The smell of alcohol on him was obvious. I figured he's drunk, but he's also a bit too aggressive for this to just be an alcohol-fueled tirade. I mean, he's switching personalities like Sybil. There's got to be pills or something else involved here.

Now I started to worry that his hands were free. I kept looking forward but have one eye on him at all times. I see his hand moving and again I knock it away.

"Do not touch your seat belt."

"Are you a cop?"

"No."

"Then why are you doing this to me? What did I do to you?"

"You're bugging me, that's why. You're going to take away from my time at home. You made the stewardess wake me up. You made me give up my nice seat in first class. So just sit there and shut up or these folks are going to put you under arrest, then you'll go to jail. If you don't say another word, we're going to let you go your own way when we land. You can enjoy Vegas and I can go home and have fun with my family."

He took a deep breath. "F you."

Oh boy, this guy was classic. Now I don't want to alarm the other passengers, but I also want to let this guy know that I'm not putting up with his shit. I turned my head to look him in the eye and quietly say, "Great, f you, too."

Now he's getting louder. And he's punching the seat in front of him. He's screaming. He rips off his seat belt, stands up, puts his finger in my face and yells, "F you!" again, just in case I missed it the first three times.

After he got that out, I hit him in the stomach. He doubled over in pain and I hit him in the face. That put him right back down in the seat. I jumped up out of my seat—so did Special Forces—and we grabbed him. With one hand on his neck, the other on the seat of his pants, we spun him around and sent him headfirst into the cart again. He crumpled to the ground. Here comes the lady with the zip ties again.

This time I'm not talking her out of it.

We put one zip tie around each hand, then zipped

those together. He's sitting up against the food cart and starting to squirm. The stewardess was nervous that he was moving around, but I assured her that with me standing in front of him, blocking any path to the main cabin, he wasn't going anywhere.

The phone in the back rings. It was the pilot wanting to know what was going on. She explained that for the safety of all the passengers we had to arrest him and now have him restrained. She then listened to what the pilot had to say for about a minute and hung up.

"The pilot says he's going to make an emergency landing in Phoenix."

Phoenix? This was not going to work for me.

"No! Call him back . . . we don't need to go to Phoenix. Look, I've got him under control. Let's just please go right to Vegas. I need to get home and see my family. Please, I do not want to stop in Phoenix."

She called back and convinced the pilot that I was on top of the situation, making an emergency landing in Phoenix unnecessary. The pilot agreed, but insisted I fill out an incident report. Now this guy is still screaming and squirming, but I figure I can do some paperwork while he acts like an idiot. Then he started spitting at me and trying to reach my pant leg to pull me down.

I glared down and let him know, "That's it. Now my patience is gone." Being a bodyguard and a cop earlier in my life, I know how to do certain things to restrain dangerous individuals without having to use my hands.

What I did to this guy was turn him on his stomach, pick his arms up, and step on his neck. What this does is pull everything forward and cut off the airway on the top. So I'm standing on top of him, he can't breathe, and I'm filling out the report.

Special Forces now comes over and tells me, "His lips are . . . his whole face is red."

"I know that."

"His lips are blue now."

"I'm aware of that, Special Forces."

"I think you better get off him."

"And I think you better shut up. This is between me and him now."

"His eyes are rolling back in his head."

"Yes, this move will do that."

What I was doing was taking the fight out of him. About thirty seconds later I feel his body completely relax. This meant he was almost ready to pass, but not quite there. I dropped my leg and picked him up. He's coughing violently, trying to get his breath back. The fight was gone.

We are now fifteen minutes from landing.

I have him sit up on the floor, with his back against he cart. I don't want to move him again until we land, so I tell the stewardess to take my seat and I'll use their seats in the back with him under my legs so he can't go anywhere.

"Sorry, sir, but we can't have that. It would be against Federal Aviation rules. He needs to be in a regulation seat."

"A regulation seat? You've got to be kidding me here."

"No, sir. Those are the rules."

The last thing I wanted to do at this time was have an argument with the stewardess, especially one over where everyone was going to sit. So I get him vertical and drag him back to the seats in the last row.

Even though he's handcuffed and his hands are behind

his back, he tries to spin to one side, reach around, and undo the seat belt. Somehow during all of this he puts his hand between the two seats and cuts his hand on something. Now he's bleeding all over the place.

I don't know if he's got hepatitis, HIV, jaundice, or whatever. Special Forces gets a towel to compress it and the guy starts screaming again. I put my hand over his mouth and he tries to bite me. I pull my hand away and he acts like he's about to spit on me.

When I see this, I reach across the aisle, grab a blanket, and throw it over his head. It was funny to see this guy acting real tough while he's got a blanket on his head.

He screams out *"You . . ."* and before he can get anything else out I put my hand over where his mouth is so his yelling is all muffled. He can't bite me now because of the blanket so my hand is safe.

I could feel when he wanted to take a breath and I'd let go, then cover up his mouth before he could finish what he wanted to scream, so every time it was just *"You . . ."*

I actually thought this was real funny in a cartoonish kind of way, so I'm sort of chuckling, getting a kick out of this. The rest of the passengers all know what's going on, but no one would turn around and look. I think they were all just so scared.

When we got to the airport we had emergency clearance so all the other planes got out of our way; we cruise right in. While we're on the ground taxiing, the stewardess walks over to us.

"The pilot wants to know what you would like to do."

"Well, this is just my advice, it's his plane, but when we come to a stop I would tell everyone to remain in their seats. Everyone already knows what's going on here, so you're not alarming them. Let the cops come in and get him off first."

The pilot agreed and made the announcement. Everyone cooperated.

Here come the police, who are joined by one federal guy. As they're making their way down the aisle I still have the blanket on this guy's head. Special Forces says, "You should take the blanket off his head now."

"And you should keep quiet, I'm not having him spit on me again. I know what I'm doing."

The federal guy, who was in charge of the group, gets to us first and asks, "Why is there a blanket on this man's head?"

"Because he tried to spit on me, then bite me."

"Oh, is that so?" The federal agent removed the blanket and got right in our guy's face. "You try to spit on me and I'll knock all your teeth out. I am not as nice as these gentlemen."

That set their relationship up right off the bat and I'm thinking, "I like this guy!"

So they get him up and we're all walking him out and the rest of the plane gave us this big standing ovation as a thank you. When we get out by the gate, the media is all there, cameras, reporters. Now, I don't want to be anywhere near this story. I just wanted to get home.

Delta has been so great to me since that flight. They hooked me up with tons of free miles. The crew who was on the flight was Las Vegas based, so I see them a lot when I fly home. They put me in first class whenever they can now. It's great. I also see the federal agent, Bill, who I like a lot. I saw him just last week actually and we were joking about me causing problems on planes.

The next time I flew with that flight crew, I asked the stewardess why, with a plane full of people, she woke me up, it's not like I was the biggest guy on the flight.

"Because I know you're a WWE wrestler. I figured you had to know some takedown moves."

Usually, people are just looking for an autograph or a picture when they recognize me.

A Samoan, a Car Accident, and a Coincidence

Dr. Tom Prichard

Back in the early eighties, one of the territories I worked was Pensacola. It consisted of Mobile, Birmingham, Dothen, and mid-Pensacola.

There was one run where Samu, Afa's son, rode with me in my Honda Prelude from Atlanta to Birmingham. We worked our matches in Alabama, and then headed out to stay at Samu's place in Pensacola. I was at the wheel, and at one point along the way, I reached for something in the backseat. As I searched for it, Samu yelled, "Watch out!"

His warning came too late and we hit a car that was abandoned on the side of the freeway. Another guy and his girlfriend stopped behind us just to see if we were all right. The cops came about a minute after this nice couple. The police were asking everyone what happened so they could fill out a report. As the gentleman who pulled in behind us was explaining to the cop what he'd seen, another guy pulled over by us but he wasn't interested in helping out—he started hitting on the other guy's girlfriend!

It was pretty clear that this guy was drunk so the cop arrested him for DUI.

The couple who stopped to help asked if there was anything they could do for us. Since it was so late at night and we knew we wouldn't be able to get a rental car until the morning, we took them up on their offer. Samu and I ended up going back to their place and crashing on their couches.

Think about how generous this was of them. We were quite a pair—a crazy-looking, large Samoan and a whacked-out kid—and they opened their home to us.

The next morning the guy took us to the rental car place and we went on to Mobile to wrestle. I made sure to get this couple's address so I could send them a thank-you letter and gift for all they did.

Once I finished that wrestling tour and got back home, things happened and I never sent them anything.

Four years later, I was at a bar in Birmingham having some beers after a show. This woman kept looking over at me. I thought she was checking me out, so I decided to play it cool and just stay where I was.

She finally came over to me and asked, "Excuse me, are you a wrestler?" I proudly told her I was, thinking she'd be impressed with what I did for a living.

"Did you wreck your car on the side of the road in Birmingham a few years ago?"

"Yeah, I did. How do you know that?"

"My boyfriend and I stopped behind you to make sure you and your friend were okay. You guys ended up staying at our place that night."

What a small world it is. Never in a million years did I think I'd ever see these folks again. We ended up talking for a bit that night, she told me that her and the man who stopped with her were still together and all was going well with them.

It was nice to see this woman again, but in the end I felt like a big schmuck for never sending them anything for their generosity.

He Sticks the Landing

Brooklyn Brawler

When I first started traveling with Harvey Whipple-man he used to always wear a baseball cap. For some reason I've always hated baseball caps. I don't know why for sure. I think it's because I just associate them with punks. Like when I think about what a wise guy looks like, I figure he'll be wearing a baseball hat.

So anyway, one day we were going down the highway, I was driving, Harvey was in the passenger seat. We were talking and all of a sudden I got real annoyed with his cap. I roll down the electronic window on his side, rip his hat off, and throw it out the window. I didn't say a word. I just looked at him for a second.

Now, you figure most people would get hot; not Harvey. He opened the door while the car was going, jumped out, rolled over three times when he hit the ground, picked himself up, pounced on the hat, and came limping back to the car. I pulled over to the shoulder the second he fell out because I had no idea what was going on.

The first thing out of his mouth when he gets back to the car was, "How did I look?"

I'm like, "How did you look? I don't know how you looked. What did you do that for?"

"I wanted my hat."

He jumped out of a speeding car because he didn't want to lose this cheap hat—that was his only explanation for nearly killing himself. I know I shouldn't have thrown it out there for no reason, but he really shouldn't have thrown himself into danger like that.

My biggest fear was that he would break his leg in the jump. Then we'd go to TV and Vince would ask how it happened and we'd have to explain it. I don't think Vince would have found that story too funny at the time.

Lita

On my birthday in 2003, we had Monday Night *Raw* in the Allstate Arena in Chicago. The girls gave me a huge birthday cake after my match with Trish Stratus that night. We ate some of the cake, but the majority of it was untouched.

I felt bad just letting it go to waste, so I brought it with us to a nearby diner where we ate after the show. There were a ton of fans that had just been to the show and were asking for pictures and autographs. We had asked if they wouldn't mind waiting until we were done eating and we'd sign for them then.

By the time we were done eating, there were probably close to a hundred fans waiting for pictures and autographs. I went through about twenty people, and then decided to spice it up a little. I told each person they could only get their picture with me if they'd wear birthday cake icing on their nose for the picture.

It was all in good fun and everyone was excited about their icing-on-the-nose pictures. Midway through this im-promptu autograph session, a teenage boy told me that not only could I put icing on his nose, but I could smash the whole cake in his face!

I told him to sit tight, I'd take him up on the offer. After finishing up the whole line, I offered a piece of cake to anyone who was interested. That left us with about half. Then Matt got out his video camera, all of the fans sang "Happy Birthday" to me, and at the end of the song, I threw the cake in the volunteer's face! Cake went flying every-where.

As we're all cracking up looking at the mess, Matt asked me if I "was sure that they said this was okay to do."

"Sure, he volunteered for it!"

"No, not the kid," Matt said. "I'm talking about the restaurant. Look around, there's cake everywhere!"

Great question. I hadn't really thought that part through.

When we realized we might be in for a long night if we stuck around, we left money on the table and got out of there right away. There is probably still evidence in the carpet of that place. Part of me wants to go back and check, but the other part of me says it's probably better to find a new diner in that town.

Flying Milk? That's Odd

Al Snow

Marty Jannetty was a great guy to travel with. He was always up to something, so life on the road never got boring with him around.

The way we used to do some of the tours a few years ago was we would do a run in one area and stay in the same town the whole time. For example, we'd do a run through upstate New York, stay in Albany the whole time, and travel to all the buildings from there. That would be our home base. It's never easy making a hotel your home, so we had to find ways to entertain ourselves.

There was this one time with Marty, and I forget who we were rooming with, but there were three of us staying in the room so we had a roll-away cot. I went in to take a shower and, first off, I go to tear back the shower curtain and the whole thing just rips right off. Marty had actually taken the time to unclip all the clips on the shower curtain and then place them back up so gingerly that the first touch would make the whole thing drop.

Then he'd stuffed the showerhead full of Vaseline or something like that so as soon as I turned on the water, I'm suddenly covered with hot water and petroleum jelly. I have no idea where he ever came up with that one; it was nothing I'd ever heard of.

Later that same day, I'm back in the bathroom and I knew something was going on outside in the room. From the sounds I was able to pick up, I couldn't tell exactly what was going on, but I knew he was hatching something. Like I said, he was always up to something.

So I open the bathroom door and take a step back. Thank God I did because a half-gallon of milk comes flying past me and slams up against the wall. I'm trying to figure out how the hell he did that, because right now there was no one in the room to throw it.

I walk out of the bathroom doorway and saw that he had taken the mattress off the roll away and somehow wedged it between the door and the wall, placed the milk on top of it and fixed it so that when I moved the door it would act like a catapult. Launching the milk across the room.

He was constantly coming up with this stuff. It just never ended with him. But like I said, it helped make sure life on the road never got boring.

This Really Works Your Shoulders

Steven Richards

When I was spending some time training at the camp in Ohio, I was driving home from wrestling school one day with Bill DeMott and Tommy Dreamer. We were on this busy road near where we lived, driving behind this bus. The three of us were busy talking about something that happened that morning at camp when we see the bus crash into an overpass bridge. You know, the kind of thing that people can walk over to get across a highway.

We pulled over right away and start running to it. It was a commuter bus, so it's packed. Because of where the bus was stopped, its right side was sort of pressed up against the bridge, you couldn't open the front door, so we're helping people out through the windows.

As we were getting the bus driver out, he said to us, "Man, I can't believe I fell asleep at the wheel. I am tired, though. I think I stayed up a little too late last night drinking." We didn't know if he was kidding or what his deal was.

We eventually got everyone out and helped people call their families on cell phones and got everyone in an ambulance who needed one. Fortunately, there were no major injuries; everyone was okay. The bus driver, to his credit, admitted to the cops when they showed up that he was completely responsible for the accident because he fell asleep. He could have made up some story if he wanted to, but he didn't. He owned right up to it.

There actually was a funny part to all of this, too. We had just about everyone off the bus, and when we went back in to see who was left, there was one more woman. Let's just say this woman was big-boned.

Tommy was in front of Bill and I, so he noticed her first. When he did, he looked back at us with the funniest expression, like, "What the hell are we going to do here." It felt like someone had written this comedy scene for us.

After a few attempts, we realized the only thing we

could do was to have Tommy and Bill each grab a leg and put me in the back to hold her steady in case she started to fall back.

It took us a while, but we got her out of there. And we got our afternoon workout.

Life on the road means moments
like these are few; the youngest
Dudleys— D-Von's sons.

The Sacrifice

"There have been times on the road when I've broke down. Just listening to my kid saying, 'Daddy, I miss you. I wish you were here.' It's like a big knife jabbing into your heart."

—DEAN MALENKO

A few hours a week. That's what most people give up in order to get to their job. Yes, sitting in traffic every night can be frustrating, but at least you know that when it's over, you will be home with your family. Traffic is the least of what each WWE Superstar must overcome to get to work. In order to have this career, they must make extraordinary sacrifices—and ask their families to make them as well. They readily admit it is nearly impossible to deal with at times. Then they'll tell you that despite the challenges, they could never imagine doing anything else with their lives.

Not being able to witness the birth of their first child. The inability to take a sick day. Accepting the fact that their marriage will be much more challenging than a usual one. That's all part of their "commute."

The Nature Boy Cracks

Ric Flair

In the mid-eighties, I wrestled every day. I'm not saying that as a figure of speech, I mean I literally worked every day. Whenever I had a vacation, someone in Puerto Rico or somewhere like that would call me. Every time I had some time off from the [National Wrestling] Alliance, another group would call and say, "We'd like to have Flair for a big show." And I'd always take it. This went on for about four years, where I didn't have a day off the whole time.

If I look back, it's the only thing I regret about the business, not taking more time off to see my kids. The job didn't permit it. It got to me a few times.

I was doing a run through Florida one time, and wrestled an hour match for a week straight. One night, after the last show in the territory, I was driving home from Orlando and my heart started racing. I called my dad—it was about two in the morning. My dad was a doctor, and I told him, "Hey Dad, my heart's skipping beats. I don't know what's going on here."

Now, I'd been wrestling every night and also drinking hard, partying, living the lifestyle. So my dad asked, "When's the last time you slept?" And I didn't have an answer. His point was that I needed to slow it down and take it easy.

Unfortunately, I had to fly to Japan the next day. I knew that while I was over there I was scheduled to wrestle two-hour draws every night against their top two stars. It was going to be a long, tough trip. I drank the whole flight over and actually talked myself into quitting. I decided that as soon as I landed I was going to get right back on a plane and head back home. I was quitting. That's it. I couldn't do it anymore. It was all too much. I had gotten myself so worked up on the trip over that I was a complete wreck when I got there.

As soon as we landed, I heard them paging me. The head promoter's wife came to pick us up and I heard them calling for "Ric Flair" over the speaker throughout the airport in Tokyo. I looked around and thought, "I gotta get out of here before someone notices me."

I found the gate agent and asked when the next flight was leaving for Chicago. She said not for five hours, but there was a flight leaving for Seattle out of the next gate in twenty minutes. I bought a ticket and got on the plane. I didn't even wait for my bags.

I flew all the way back to Seattle, then got on another plane for Charlotte. I'm the World Champion and I'm MIA to everyone back in Japan. I was supposed to defend my title and no one there had any idea where I was.

I totally cracked when I got off the plane in Charlotte. Cracked. My wife and Jimmy Crockett were waiting for me. They told me I had to go back and wrestle. They reminded me that I was the World Champion, I was advertised to wrestle and had a responsibility to go back.

They were right. I turned around and flew all the way back to Tokyo right away. I landed two hours before the show started, got to the building pretty much right before I was supposed to go on, and went out there and wrestled for two hours.

After the show I went out drinking with some of the other guys. I got over it pretty quickly, but I just cracked there. It all just became too much for me to handle.

All the traveling and constant working pushed me to a state of mental exhaustion. I just cracked.

The Life I Know

Chavo Guerrero

Growing up in the business, I know we have it easy. I hear some of the boys complaining at times: "I'm tired. We've been on the road for two weeks." Big deal.

I grew up in a time where I didn't see my dad for six months straight; he'd be working in Japan all that time. Back then it was all different independent territories, and rather than move us around to where he worked—moving us to Florida, moving us to New York, moving us to Georgia, moving us to wherever he was at—my father was kind enough to let us stay at our home in California.

It was give and take. I missed my father a lot but I was able to have a normal childhood. He sacrificed a lot by letting us stay in one place. He and my mom sacrificed a lot by being away from each other all the time.

It's just the nature of this business.

I knew what it was going to be like living on the road. So for us, when we're on the road for four days straight, even if it's a hard loop, that's nothing for me. I feel I was born to

SmackDown! at Budakon
Arena in Japan.

be on the road. I love it. I mean, it's real hard being away
from my wife all the time, I won't lie, but I knew that would
be a challenge when I decided to get married. And my wife
knew what kind of life she was getting into, too.

It's not only me in this business, my wife's in it. I sacrifice
a lot to be in this business and my wife sacrifices a lot for us to
be in this business, too. It's a sacrifice the whole family has to
make, this business has fed my family for almost seventy years,
that's a long time man. It's a way of life and I've never known
anything different. It's what my whole family knows.

My grandmother, mother, and aunt all pulled my wife
aside at different times before our wedding and asked if she

really knew what she was getting into. They told her, "You're going to be a wrestler's wife and this is how it's going to be. You need to know that." They laid it all out for her honestly. She listened to them, so she knew. And she was willing to make the sacrifices. It's still hard for her, though.

I remember one tour about a year ago that was a tough trip. We had real bad weather in Canada, which meant a lot of delays in the airport, horrible driving conditions, I mean, everything about this trip was tougher than usual. On the last day, the boys were beat. You could see it in their faces, their body language. I remember J.R. was going around talking to all the boys, making sure everyone was going to be able to give the fans one last great show before this run ended. He came over to me and asked how I was holding up. I looked at him and said, "You know, J.R., I hear a lot of the boys complaining about it, but I grew up in your time."

He knew what that meant. He smiled, patted me on the back, and went on his way,

I don't care how hard these four days were, it was nothing compared to what my dad and the older guys went through. This trip would have been a vacation for them.

Double the pleasure, Double the pain

A-Train

I had no idea of the amount of travel this job entailed. And when I talk to the veterans and hear what they endured back in the day, it was probably three, four times more. So I have no right to complain.

The first few months I was in WWE it was like I was a

freshman in college again. I loved it. I was traveling, seeing the world, meeting new people, doing a job I absolutely loved. Nothing about it could be wrong. But then after a while it wore on me. Getting home on a Wednesday, having to leave again on a Friday after you just finished unpacking and cleaning, then you gotta pack all over and leave again. It was a tough adjustment.

My body started to get sore. I was getting sick a lot because of the air I was breathing on planes and stuff. My knees and my back hurt more and more from spending a lot of time in small spaces in planes and cars. Then, after a four-hour flight, you gotta deal with the rental cars and the airline losing your bag. People started to recognize me from TV and stopping me everywhere. There was a point where I had a real tough time dealing with it. But I just pushed through it.

I'm used to it now. Do I wish it were easier? Sure. But when I'm in that ring it's totally worth it. If the travel was two times harder I'd take that two times harder, you know what I mean? When I step through those ropes and hear the fans, man, I'd go through anything for that feeling.

Oh My, How the Times Have Changed

Jim "J.R." Ross

My early days, driving seventeen hundred miles every week, was a real challenging time. But when I look back on it I see that it taught me a lot, too. That experience allows me to fully appreciate where I am today. I believe that you truly can't appreciate where you are until you understand where you've been. When I think about where we all were business-wise years ago, it really makes me appreciate where we are today.

A lot of these new guys, they don't know how lucky they got it.

We drove on one run, Jerry Brisco, Pat Patterson, and I, about a hundred miles from Baltimore over to Harrisburg, Pennsylvania. Then we went another hundred from Harrisburg to Wilkes-Barre. From there it was about 175 to Albany the last night.

As we were riding along, we all started laughing because somehow we realized that each of us had conversations that day with people who said, "That's a hell of a drive you guys got tonight. Three hours after the show? Gosh, I'm sorry." We were all laughing because we knew that back in the day it was not unusual to make six-, seven-, even eight-hour trips after a night of making only forty bucks. This three hours from Pennsylvania to Albany was nothing.

Another area where the generational division shows is with the hotels. I remember always sharing a room with four other guys for a ten-dollar-a-night room rate. This wasn't like in the roaring twenties; it wasn't too long ago. And because I was one of the younger guys on most trips, I always slept on the floor. Sometimes I'd get a filthy hotel bedspread to cover up.

We were heading on an international trip with the WWE in 2003 and there were a limited number of rooms at the hotel. So we approached the talent about the possibility of sharing rooms for one night at this real nice hotel.

Forget that up until a few years ago, wrestlers sharing hotel rooms was the rule, but even when I did Atlanta Falcons football, as is common with every NFL team, pretty much all of the guys had roommates. The starting quarterback stays with his backup and so on.

Well, you would have thought we talked to our guys about becoming communists. It got a horrible reaction from some of them. They couldn't believe there was a chance they might have to share a room with somebody. They were like, "What if this guy snores? What if he passes gas? What if I want to get in the shower first? What if he doesn't put the toilet seat down?"

And this is all coming from the younger guys. The veterans who have been around for a while could care less about that stuff, having to share rooms with another and all. I'll tell you, a lot of the younger guys really don't know how good they've got it.

Sacramento, Reno, Sacramento, Reno

Stacy Keibler

I know I have a cool job. I go on road trips with my friends, perform for my fans in a different city pretty much every week, and then have the opportunity to see what the city has to offer.

But life on the road isn't always easy.

When you have a job that requires you to fly anywhere from two to five times each week, stay in different hotels each night, book rental cars and find your way from city to city, there are bound to be some problems.

We travel so frequently and our turnaround from one place to the next is so quick that sometimes I don't know where I am when I wake up in the morning. There was one time, where I had a bad case of "Where am I?"

After our Divas shoot in Phoenix two years ago, I was dropped off at the airport to head to my next assignment. And I was exhausted. All week we woke up at 4 A.M. to start the day and worked the whole way through.

My schedule was to fly to an autograph signing, then be driven to the house show about 130 miles away. So I had a pretty busy day ahead. The woman checking me in asked for my last name. After a brief moment of staring at the computer, she asked if I was going to Sacramento and I said yes.

I boarded the plane, fell asleep almost immediately, and didn't wake up the entire flight. When I picked up my bags, I didn't see anyone from the limo company to drive me to the signing. I waited a while, and decided to call our talent relations department. They called the limo company to find out what was going on and the limo company said they were waiting outside.

I walked out there, but did not see them anywhere. By this time we were all on the phone together. The limo company, our talent relations department, and me. I was telling them what I was wearing, where I was standing, and we still couldn't find each other.

After a little more discussion, we figured out the problem. I was in the wrong city!

I was supposed to be in Reno, but I was actually in Sacramento. This was where our house show was later that night and I guess the office had double booked me two tickets—one to go directly to the house show from the Divas shoot and one for my autograph appearance in Reno.

When the woman asked if I was going to Sacramento I

said yes without even checking my itinerary. Who ever has two different tickets waiting for them?!

It was still early in the day, so I had a choice. I could get a ride to Reno to do the appearance or I could just stay in Sacramento and wait for the house show. I was so tired, but I thought about the fans who sometimes drive two hundred miles just to see us and shake our hands, and that maybe someone drove all that way to get to Reno just to meet me. I couldn't let that person down.

I knew I had to go. My only real option for a ride was to jump in a cab. This wasn't going to be the typical "Can you take me to my hotel downtown, please?" Oh no. This was "Can you drive me the 130 miles to Reno, please?"

Fortunately, the first driver I flagged down agreed to drive me all the way there, and it was the most expensive cab ride I have ever been on!

I made it there a little late, signed for everyone, and jumped right into the limo that was now waiting for me in Reno to head back to Sacramento for the show.

After the show was over we drove to the next town. Guess what it was? You got it—Reno! Since that trip, I've never gotten on another plane without double-checking my itinerary.

Pain, Suffering, and Styrofoam

Molly Holly

On Friday, October 10, 2003, we started a run in Guelph, Ontario, and I was feeling real congested. I had a runny nose and my ears were bothering me, they were a little sore and plugged up. I wrestled the show in Guelph and felt horrible after the match.

I went right back to my hotel room and tried to get some rest. We were flying out to St. John's, New Foundland, early the next morning and I thought if I could at least get a good six hours of sleep before we left, I'd be all right. Even with some sleep, I felt just as miserable when I woke up. And it was about to get worse.

For the entire plane ride I felt like there were ice picks on each side of my head stabbing into my eardrums. I have never been in that much pain for that long a time in my life. And coming from a professional wrestler, I think that says a lot. I cried for the entire ten minutes it took to land. I could not get rid of the pain.

I tried everything to ease the pain a bit—yawning, stretching my mouth, all sorts of stuff. Nothing was working. After we landed and I was on the ground for a few minutes, the pain subsided a little, but it had traumatized me so much that it took me about an hour to pull myself together. While everyone else was getting their bags, I was off in the corner, crying in despair over what I'd just gone through.

Our trainer, who was on the flight with us, noticed me crying off on the side. I explained to him what was going on and that the pain was a lot less now. He thought that was a good sign, but told me to go to the pharmacy as soon as I got my rental car. The pharmacist recommended eardrops and some Sudafed. I took them both and got ready to wrestle that night in St. John's.

It's amazing how, when you're out there performing in the ring, you can block everything out and focus on the match. Whether it's pain or some other issue, you can concentrate only on what you need to do. After the match I was coughing so hard that my lungs hurt. My nose didn't stop running long enough to wipe it. Once again, I thought if I could only get a couple of hours of sleep before we had to leave the next day, I'd be all right.

We were actually scheduled for two flights the next day. First we were going to fly into Moncton, New Brunswick, then out later that same day to get to the Mohegan Sun Casino in Connecticut. I was dreading it. How could I handle being in that much pain again? And twice no less.

While we waited to take off the first time, I told one of the stewardesses what I went through the day before. She shared an old stewardess trick with me that she promised would help me out.

"What you do is, during takeoff and landing, stuff two hot towels into a Styrofoam coffee mug and hold them against your ears like this," She covered both ears with her hands as she said it to demonstrate. "They say the humidity helps lessen the pain."

There was no question it looked ridiculous. It was like when you were a little kid and you connected two cups with a long string, then pretended to talk into one end while your friend put the other cup up to her ear, like it was a telephone. Here I was, a grown woman, holding two Styrofoam cups over my ears.

As crazy as I looked, though, I have to admit, the pain was less than the day before. Maybe the humidity did its thing, or maybe I just convinced myself it didn't hurt as much, either way, that trick kind of worked for me.

I managed to get through my match Sunday afternoon in Moncton, then got on a plane headed for Connecticut.

And you know I had two Styrofoam cups over my ears for takeoff and landing!

When I got to the Mohegan Sun I went right in to see the doctor. After a quick look, he told me I had an ear infection in both ears. He warned me that both my eardrums could burst if I got back on a plane. It was great to find out what was wrong, I appreciated his advice, but I was scheduled to fly out Tuesday morning for Louisville to attend the OVW training camp they have there on Thursdays.

I didn't want to completely ignore what he said, so I called the airline and paid $100 to move my flight back. This way I could stay in Connecticut one more day; maybe my ears would heal by then.

Monday was a live *Raw*. I figured I'd have a title match, I was the Women's Champion at the time, but they actually gave me something much worse.

They scheduled me to do guest commentary.

So here I am unable to hear anything thanks to infections in both my ears and not really able to talk because of a severe sore throat, and I'm about ten hours away from making my debut as a guest commentator on live television. There was no way I was going to whine to Vince, "Thanks for the chance, Vince, but I'm too sick to commentate tonight. Maybe next week." That wasn't even an option.

I decided to suck it up and hope that when showtime came around, I'd feel better. I didn't talk all day, thinking I needed to "save" all the voice I had. Well, I went out there and did it. But it didn't go so well.

When I was done, the number one comment everyone had was that they couldn't hear me. That made sense, I couldn't even hear myself. I could only faintly hear J.R. and Lawler in my headset, so it was difficult to react to what they were saying to me, and with my throat so scratchy, I sounded bad, too.

I stayed in Connecticut the extra day and flew into Louisville with Styrofoam cups on my ears on Wednesday. I still felt miserable, still couldn't hear. Thursday I wrestled at their training camp in the morning and on Friday I just couldn't take the pain anymore.

I went to another doctor, this one in Louisville.

"How closely did this other doctor look at your ears?" he asked.

"Not very close, to be honest. I mean, he was the doctor at the arena and they were pretty much just looking out for sprained ankles and things like that."

"Well, let me explain to you what's going on here. The infection has completely closed off the tubes in your ears. It formed an abscess against the eardrum in your right ear that may need to be surgically removed."

"This is not what I want to hear, Doc."

"So you can either schedule a surgery or deal with it for a while until it goes away on its own."

Presented with those two choices, I knew which route I was going. I couldn't choose the surgery because I had to work, and if I had surgery I wouldn't be able to fly for awhile. I knew our upcoming schedule and knew the shows weren't within driving distance. I needed to fly.

There was nothing I could do.

So until it went away on its own or I had time for the surgery, I was just going to have to deal with being partially deaf in my right ear.

I was also going to have to deal with being the person you saw on the plane holding two Styrofoam cups over her ears.

No Nine-to-Five Gig

Dean Malenko

Friends I grew up with, friends who know me from outside of the business, always tell me they're jealous of me. "You get to travel and see the world" is what I hear all the time. They see this business only as glamorous and fun; what they don't know is the sacrifice and dedication it takes to be a part of it.

That's why you have to love this business if you're going to succeed. But it's not only you who has to make sacrifices, it's your entire family.

The divorce rate among the boys is sky high. It takes a certain person as a spouse to make a marriage with someone in this business work. I remember when I got married I was working in Japan and after my first year I got a contract with WCW that took me on the road for a lot of consecutive days on end. My wife wasn't prepared for it. She thought she was. But there's the idea of being prepared for it and then the reality of it. When that reality hits, it's tough.

So many times when we're on the road and things go wrong, we try to tell our loved ones, "You don't know how hard this is." What we forget is how hard *they* have it. I've got a wife at home who's raising two kids by herself, basically as a single mom. Now *that's* hard.

We never ask the fans to look at this end of it, we're out their to entertain them, to give them a great show, but it's interesting if you look past the glitz and glamour and see what the guys have to go through on a regular basis. The sacrifices they make with their family to be out there entertaining.

Missing a baby's first steps, a football game, a ballet recital. Unlike football or other sporting events where guys get six months off to be at home, we go all the time, year-round.

There have been times on the road when I've broken down, you know? Just listening to my kid saying, "Daddy, I miss you. I wish you were here." It's like a big knife jabbing into your heart.

At the same time, I'm a second-generation wrestler and my dad was on the road for thirty years, so I had to go through it as a kid, too. That experience got me prepared for dealing with this side of it.

And what's the alternative? Sitting at a desk for a nine-to-five? I couldn't do that and my wife knows it. Not that I'd even be qualified to do anything anyway besides this business . . . it's still my choice to do this.

And the sacrifice is worth it.

When you're in a building with tens of thousands of screaming fans and you and whoever you're working with that night have the ability to incite laughter, cheers, anger . . . there's just nothing like that in the world. To have twenty thousand people applauding what you do. You can have a nine-to-five job and have a boss slap you on the back and say, "Hey, great job." I know that's good at times, but there's nothing like the feedback you get from an arena full of fans for doing something you've been working so hard at for years.

You can have a tough couple of months on the road, be real tired, but that one night when you go out there and give everything you've got and the fans applaud you, man, you'll sit back in the dressing room with a smile on your face and realize it's all worth it. All the starving, all the working for hot dogs and sodas, driving five hundred miles and sharing a hotel room with five other guys. It's all worth it when you reach that top point of your career.

Once you get that, it's hard to go back the other way.

How could you go from entertaining millions of fans to an office job or working retail?

five

Strange Meeting You Here

"Santa Claus was a Mattitude follower and an
Edgehead, which was pretty cool."
—EDGE

Have you ever been waiting to board a plane and noticed a

celebrity being whisked through the airport, or on your

flight, en route to their next engagement? Whether it's the

latest box-office star or that guy from the cell phone com-

mercial whose name you don't know but you've seen him

on TV, there's a good chance you've had a celebrity airport

run-in. ⚙ With the WWE Superstars crisscrossing the

globe on a regular basis, you know they're bound to bump

into some famous folks along the way, and most celebrity

sightings take place on a plane. There is one run-in that

went down only after two Superstars took a wrong turn and ended up in front of you-know-who's North Pole hideaway.

From holiday icons to world leaders, the Superstars have seen them all. But when a famous sports entertainer whose face is known all over the world runs into another celebrity . . . who's more excited to see who?

This Really Is First Class

Sergeant Slaughter

I took my former wife, Diane, on a run of Southern California once. We stayed for a couple of days after the shows were done to sightsee around Los Angeles. On the way home, we were booked in first class on a Pan Am flight, it was a huge plane, a 747.

Because we bought her ticket a couple of weeks after mine, we had separate seats. The way this first-class cabin was set up is it had four rows on each side. The first row had only one seat, then there were two in the next three rows. My ticket was for the single seat in the front row.

I asked the guy at the ticket counter if I could sit with my wife. He said that I should just sit with her when we get on the plane and when the person booked for that seat boarded, just ask them if they would mind switching seats with me. It seemed easy enough, so we got right on. The plane was delayed for a while, and we sat together relaxing, reading the newspaper. There was no one else in the first-class cabin at this point.

Then some guy, who didn't work for the airline, walked over and asked to see my ticket.

"You're supposed to be sitting a few rows up, sir."

"Yeah, I know. We're trying to see if we could switch around so I can sit with my wife."

"No sir, you have to sit in that seat," and he pointed to the single row in front.

My ego was kind of crushed at this point. I was hoping maybe he might know who I was and it would help me, but this guy was intense about the seating arrangements.

"You have to go sit in that seat right now, sir."

Not wanting to make a scene, I got up and sat in the front row. I was so annoyed. I was too mad to even read the paper so I just stared at the wall in front of me. Then I heard a ruckus behind me, like there were a lot of people getting on the plane at the same time. I refused to turn around to see what was going on. I wasn't about to give them the satisfaction of my attention because they took my seat.

Pretty soon my wife was frantically tapping me on the shoulder. "Bob, Bob, you'll never guess who's on the plane."

"Who?"

She leaned down and whispered in my ear, "Former President Nixon."

"Oh yeah."

"He's sitting right behind you."

"Okay."

I mean, I was still so annoyed about that guy not switching seats with me that I really didn't care who was on this plane with me. Former president or not, I wanted to sit with my wife.

She went back to her seat and was soon joined by a Secret Service guy in the seat that I wanted, next to her. He was just staring straight ahead, when all of a sudden he said out loud to himself, "That's Sgt. Slaughter up there. I can't believe Sgt. Slaughter is on the plane."

He turned to my wife and asked her, "Do you know who Sgt. Slaughter is? Well, he's sitting right there."

My wife started to laugh and told the agent, "Yes, I know him. I'm his wife. And you're actually sitting in his seat right now."

"Really? Oh boy, I'd do anything to talk to him. Hey, once we get going, would you mind switching seats with him for a little bit so we can sit together and talk?"

My wife told him she would. So I was getting closer. I'd be in the row that I wanted, just not with the person I was hoping to sit with.

Now, I'm still annoyed, staring straight ahead at the wall. Then I heard a voice speaking quietly behind me, "Mr. President, Mr. President . . . Sgt. Slaughter is sitting right in front of you. Sgt. Slaughter!"

"Oh yes, yes. Sgt. Slaughter." I heard him moving around and felt him pat me on the shoulder. I got up and there is President Nixon standing in front of me, giving me a big salute. I gave him one back.

"I remember when you were on TV and you beat that Iranian fellow, and turned into a good guy. Then you did the pledge of allegiance. I was watching with my grandkids and we all stood up to say it with you. It is an honor to meet such a proud American. Whatever you need, please let me know."

"It is an honor to meet you as well, sir. To be honest, I would just like to sit with my wife if that's possible. One of your agents is in my seat."

I didn't know that my wife and this Secret Service gentleman had already made plans, so she took my seat and I sat with him for a while to talk wrestling. He was a great fan.

Of course, when word got out that President Nixon and Sgt. Slaughter were in the plane, people were coming up to him and asking for his autograph and asking me for my autograph.

President Nixon asked me for two autographs for his grandkids and he took out a picture of himself and signed it for us. We all talked for the entire ride back to New York, and the moment after we touched down, they left through the side door and right into a car that was waiting for them on the runway. They were gone in an instant. The plane continued up to the gate to let the rest of us off.

This plane ride started out so badly for me, but it turned into a trip I'll always remember fondly.

Senator Nowinski?

Chris Nowinski

I had the opportunity to attend the 2004 Democratic National Convention. The whole trip was incredible, just a surreal experience—sitting in the arena watching these speeches live and feeling the energy that was coming from the delegates.

Those are some of the most hard-core party members. It was kind of a wild atmosphere to expect from politics. And just an amazing cross-section of politicians and celebrities.

I was right ahead of John Cusack in the security line. I had the chance to meet various congressmen and governors.

MSNBC did an interview with me so I had the chance to talk to Ron Reagan for a while a couple days before he spoke.

I had the opportunity to speak at a Young Democrats' summit. When I walked in, Teresa Heinz Kerry was at the podium. Following her? P. Diddy. Those were the two folks who spoke right before me.

I remember watching from the back thinking, "I have to follow P. Diddy? What the hell is going on here?!"

Britney, the Diva?

Trish Stratus

This doesn't happen often these days with how tight security is at the airports, but there was this one time when a few of the guards asked me for a couple of autographs and to pose for some pictures with them. I was only trying to be nice by signing and all, but I ended up inadvertently creating quite a buzz in the place.

The entire walk to the gate, people were asking for my autograph, which led to even more people coming up to me. I even got a few, "Can I have an autograph? Thanks . . . so who are you anyway?"

When I finally got to the gate, I grabbed a seat and was immediately approached by two security guards and an official-looking guy, who asked me if I'm okay or if I need any assistance. Just as I was telling them I was okay and it was no big deal, a group of kids headed my way to get an autograph. After I finish signing all of their stuff, the official-looking guy asked how long until my flight.

"A little over an hour."

"Great, come with me."

So he took me up some elevator, into a lounge, and made sure I was comfortable. He asked if he could get me a cool beverage and within minutes a woman brought me over the Diet Coke I requested. The official-looking guy told me to relax, that he'll come get me before my flight.

He left and the woman who brought the Diet Coke came back over to me, this time asking to see my boarding pass. She returned with a bowl of mixed nuts and a new boarding pass with a new seat—in first class.

Wow! This is great! I can get used to this living.

So I chill for an hour, read my book, and indulge in my snacks until the official-looking guy returns, accompanied by the same two security guards who first approached me, they took me the "back way" to the gate. We preboard the plane so I can get settled before anyone else comes on.

This was all so incredible. The service, the luxury, I couldn't believe what they did for me. I thanked my newly found entourage and shook their hands as I say my good-byes.

"You're very welcome, it's our pleasure," they said. "We're huge fans of yours, Ms. Spears."

Me and Jimmie V.

Jim "J.R." Ross

In the late eighties I was working with Jim Crockett Promotions. What happened at the time was Jim, who was providing NWA programming for TBS, bought out the UWF from Cowboy Bill Watts. Now, before Watts had sold, he had made a commitment for office space in Dallas, where I was living at the time. Crockett was based in Charlotte and wasn't going to move his base of operations, but he had this office space in Dallas. Crockett hired me to be a play-by-play guy and asked that I keep living in Dallas, using the office space there so it didn't go to waste.

Most of our TV tapings were in the old Mid-Atlantic area—Charlotte, Greensboro, Richmond, Norfolk—so I did a lot of traveling in and out of Dallas to the Carolina area.

Coming back from an NWA TV taping in Raleigh I had a seat in the last row of first class. One of the good things about all this traveling was that I was racking up so many miles that I could always upgrade to first class. I took my seat next to the window. A few minutes later, North Carolina State basketball coach Jim Valvano sat down next to me.

This was in, I want to say 1987, so it was a few years after he won the National Championship but before he was diagnosed with cancer. He was going to a speaking engagement out in California and was connecting via Dallas.

He and I sat together from Raleigh to Dallas—about, three, three and a half hours—and we talked the entire time. He was a fan of wrestling, he was a big Ric Flair fan especially. Flair being from the Carolinas contributed to that for sure.

He loved the theatrical aspect of what the guys did. He said, "You know, I've been known for my showmanship on the floor, too." He knew what we were doing, just having fun out there. "Sometimes you gotta go over the top to make your point no matter what industry you're in. I have to be a showman at times, too."

We also talked a lot about athletic officiating. I officiated high school and college sports for eighteen years, including college basketball. I explained to him how difficult a job it is. You go to Duke, North Carolina State, places where the emotions are intense, and you got fans sitting right on top of you.

They're young, defiant, boisterous. It's a unique environment for sure. I told him that I believed there are officials who are incompetent and shouldn't be on the floor officiating . . . but the same could be said about some coaches. The only difference is with coaches it's easy to see. Wins and losses determine that.

When I said that he jumped right in. "You put it that way and there are a lot of coaches who don't belong in Division One because they're not successful."

From there we started talking about whether or not officials let their personal feelings get in the way. I shared my belief that most officials were honest. I know I was always honest out there, but I also admitted that I didn't get every call right. I'd look back at tapes of games and see that I missed some. I'm only human. The only two things you can ask a referee for are honesty and for him to bust his ass out there. If they're lazy and they're loafing on you, you can call them on that. As for the honesty, I promised him I had never heard an official admit he was out to screw any one coach.

I remember when I got done explaining my side, he looked at me as serious as can be and said, "I've never had this civil a conversation with a basketball referee in all my life. I've never heard anyone discuss it this way." He told me he really appreciated it and was going to try and look at the officials' side a bit differently.

Another interesting thing happened while we were eating breakfast on the plane. The food was, well, we all know airlines are not known for their food, so we can leave it at that. They served us a bowl of cereal and some fruit. Like slices of orange, a piece of strawberry, and some grapes. The first thing I did was pour some Sweet 'N Low on my oranges.

"Why do you do that?" Jimmie V. asked.

"I need to sweeten up my oranges or else I'd never eat them."

"We're more alike than you know. The tartness of the orange has always kept me from eating fruit. My wife asks me to eat healthier all the time, but I tell her I can't stand the taste of it. The fruit is just too tart. I never thought of pouring Sweet 'N Low on it. Look at all I've learned from you today. Be more understanding of officials and how to eat healthier."

Jimmie V. was just a real neat guy. We exchanged phone numbers before we separated at the airport. We talked probably a handful of times on the phone after that. This was before cell phones and we both had jobs that kept us on the road all the time, so it wasn't like we could talk a lot.

I had a standing invitation to any game if we were in the area, just let him know. It was really interesting, even though I only had one plane ride with him, he was, from what I could tell, a guy who would have been a great friend over time. I truly felt that we would have had an enjoyable time building a relationship.

Then, of course, he passed away way too soon. To this day, it still brings tears to my eyes watching the clip of his speech at that awards ceremony.

And what he said that night was true. Cancer could rob him of his strength; it could rob him of a lot of things, but not his spirit. He was just a great man who I was truly fortunate to have met thanks to this business.

he Real X

Chris Jericho

During one long flight, I was watching the movie *JFK* on my computer. I got up to go to the bathroom somewhere in the middle of it and on my way back I noticed that Donald Sutherland was seated in the row right behind mine. It was kind of cool because he has an integral role in *JFK*—he plays X, the informant. It's always been one of my favorite acting roles.

At first I thought maybe my mind was playing tricks on me because I'd just seen his face in a movie and now here was someone who looked like him sitting five feet from me. I took another look at this person and decided it was definitely him.

I went over and asked him for an autograph. He gave me the typical, "Yeah, okay." Then I asked if he wouldn't mind signing the DVD case for *JFK*, I just happened to be watching it.

He thought that was pretty cool and we started talking about the role for a while. That ended up being a pretty cool plane ride.

Cuss a Priest Lately?

John "Bradshaw" Layfield

I was in Kabul, Afghanistan, on a USO tour. I had been overseas visiting our troops for about a week and a half. This was my first USO tour and our guys were still heavily involved in the war in Afghanistan. We were going to be some of the first celebrities to visit Kabul.

I love visiting our troops in the field. They are a long way from home, and they are there because they are defending our freedom. These guys are the true heroes in our society today. I was there with a big group from the Sergeant Major of the Army Jack Tilley; a terrific recording artist Darryl Worley and his guitar player Soir; Karri Turner from the TV show *Jag;* and many others. We were there to tell our guys thanks.

Most of our days were long ones. We would get up around 6 A.M. and eat with the soldiers. Then we'd get into the Blackhawk helicopters and fly to many of the forward bases and visit soldiers. When we got back from that in the late afternoon, we'd get ready for the evening performance. Once the evening performance wrapped up, we'd sign autographs until about midnight. It sounds like a tough schedule until you realize what is was we were doing: visiting the very people who make America free, and you realize that you love every minute of it.

This one morning we had gotten up early as usual and had already greeted hundreds of soldiers before we arrived in Kabul. We were flown there by two great pilots, Stan and Hutch, who I still keep in touch with.

As we walked into Kabul we saw all the damage that had just taken place in the war, the bombed barracks and the destroyed buildings. Empty shells were all over the ground because this was where a bloody battle had taken place.

Darryl Worley, Soir, and I were walking together greeting soldiers. Understand, these guys had been in a pretty bloody war, they were just glad to see anyone who wasn't carrying a gun. We were also trying to get over the flight with Stan and Hutch—we had stupidly asked them what the choppers were capable of doing. We found out it is hard to make me airsick. I think at one point we were upside down, because the tears were running into my hair.

I saw a soldier coming to me in a Santa Claus hat; this was two days away from Christmas. I thought that was cute until I realized that he was going to run over me.

I tried to disarm him as he got close and I said, "Merry Christmas, where you from?" He grabbed my hand, hit his chest to mine, and said, "Who are you?" I was pretty agitated that this guy would act like that, so I said, "Who the $%&#* are you?"

He looked at me like I had shot him and said, "I'm the chaplain, so watch your language young man!"

The Santa hat had covered up his clergy designation, and he thought he was being funny. Real funny, out of four thousand soldiers I cussed the one priest. Darryl Worley and Soir fell on the ground laughing. Everyone laughed but me and the chaplain, I tried to apologize but he didn't want to hear it. He later laughed and let me off the hook, saying he was an old tank commander and had heard worse.

At the next base in Uzbekistan the chaplain met me at the plane and told me that he had heard about me and he would be watching me.

Now, every time I see a soldier who has heard about the incident, they always ask if I've cussed a priest lately.

Well, It's the Big Ho?

Big Show

My wife, Bess, travels with me a lot of the time. She'll make the full rounds with me. Every live event, every television taping, every Pay-Per-View. These times are great because we get to spend time together and Bess gets a firsthand view of the entire business to see what the life of a Superstar truly entails.

Sometimes, though, there are even more perks.

I went through several changes with my character when I first arrived in WWE. During one of these periods, the WWE creative department was experimenting with my humorous side. I did several impressions that I had such a great time with, including Hulk Showgan, Showkishi, Showman the Barbarian, and Fat Bastard.

Although my personal favorite was the night when Vince informed me that I would be impersonating The Godfather! This of course sounded like great fun, until Vince explained that I'd have to kiss one of the "Ho's." I was totally cool with the idea of wearing gold chains, dancing and playing up the role, but the problem was me kissing another woman on a night Bess was sitting backstage.

I expressed my fear to Vince. Yes, I said fear! It doesn't matter how big I am, telling Bess that I had to kiss another woman wasn't something I was looking forward to. So I asked Vince to do it for me.

Being the confident leader that he is, Vince looked me straight in the eyes and without hesitation said, "No problem." He seemed so confident, I knew this was something I had to see.

Mr. Vincent Kennedy McMahon has always been known for his huge grapefruits, but this time he would meet his match. He had no idea what he was about to go up against. I would just as soon kick a Bengal tiger in the balls in a phone booth than tick off my wife. She isn't intimidated by anyone.

Bess, a statuesque five-foot-eleven brunette with piercing blue-gray eyes, stood off to the side of the stage as Vince approached her. They chatted for only a minute or so. I figured it didn't go well.

Vince came over to me and let me know we were all set; Bess was okay with the whole idea.

What? How?

"We're putting Bess in the show. She's going to play the woman you kiss."

Smooth, just plain smooth. I should have expected something like this from Vince. He's such a great businessman who thinks on his feet quick as a cat—and let's not forget he's also married to a formidable woman, so he totally understands the game.

So that night in Anaheim, I dressed up as a pimp and kissed my wife on national television. My wife, on the "Ho Train," how cool is that?

Of all the trips Bess has joined me on, this is still one of our favorites for sure.

Claus Is the Name, Wrestling's the Game

Edge

Our first tour of 2003 was a difficult one. Not only was the travel long—we went from Albuquerque, New Mexico, to San Francisco then up to Alaska—but this was the trip where I fully lost the strength in my arm and realized something was wrong with my neck. If not for meeting Santa Claus, this might have been one of my worst trips ever.

In Alaska, January is in the part of the year when it's like night all day. Matt [Hardy] and I were driving around Fairbanks at three in

the afternoon trying to find a gym and it's pitch black outside.

We weren't having any luck so we pulled over to a gas station. The attendant said he knew of a gym that was a little bit of a trip to get to. He gave us these directions, which put us on some desolate road with no hint of a gym anywhere. We were about to turn back when we noticed a sign that read "North Pole: 11 miles." The two of us immediately decided we had to go there. It wasn't the real North Pole, but at least we could say we were at the North Pole.

A little bit up the road we passed another sign for it. This one gave us the mile marker and also proclaimed it as "Home of the Santa Claus House." We pulled over to take pictures next to this sign. How many times in your life are you going to be in front of sign like this? We get back in the car and once we're in the area of the "North Pole" we pull into McDonald's to get some hot chocolate.

We asked the guy where Santa Claus lives, kind of jokingly, and he answered back with a straight face, "Oh, right around the corner." Huh? Really? "Yeah, just go up this road and go around the next corner and you'll see it." So we followed his directions, and sure enough, there was Santa Claus's house.

It's this great big tourist attraction; it was awesome. We go in and Santa knew who we were. Before we could say anything, he's like, "Hey, you're Matt Hardy and Edge!" He was a Mattitude follower and an Edgehead, which was pretty cool. Can you believe that? We're all excited to go see this Santa Claus house and he knows who we are. Santa took some pictures and chatted with us; this guy actually changed his name to Kris Kringle—man, he was living the whole gimmick. Then he took us out back, where he had the reindeer.

Prancer was the only one left because he had gored some of the other guys a few days before, and they hadn't had a chance to get any new ones yet. We went into the store to buy all sorts of Christmas decorations, took some more pictures, and hung out with Santa for a bit before getting on our way to make it to the show on time.

When Matt and I got to the building we started telling everyone about our trip to Santa Claus's house and no one believed us. It was like we were eight years old again, telling kids in school about how we saw Santa Claus and no one would believe us. Later on, though, Santa showed up at the building. We got him front-row seats.

I wrestled John Cena that night, and he of course did a rap on Santa. We did a spot during the match where I rammed Cena into the wall right in front of where Santa was sitting, and we gave each other the high five and everything. The crowd was so into the Santa spots. It's official: Santa Claus is so over with the fans in Alaska.

Rikishi and Chuck Palumbo rocking to the beat, just one thing to pass time on the road.

six

The Fraternity

*"I was ready to go home and see my family because
I missed them, but I'd be lying if I didn't admit I was
a little upset to be leaving those guys."*
—CHAVO GUERRERO

If you've ever gone to sleep-away camp for the summer or at-tended college and lived in the residence hall, you understand the bond you form with the people you meet there. While you're all out there on your own, away from your families, spe-cial relationships form because you all understand what every-one is going through. Miss mom's cooking? So does someone else. Having a tough time in calculus? So is the guy down the hall. There is always someone there for you, someone to lis-ten, someone who knows what you're feeling. The group you are with becomes a second family you can depend on.

WWE Superstars are the same way. The men and women they work with become so much more than the opponent they must defeat in the ring. Spending over two hundred days each year on the road and away from their real families, they form special relationships and bonds with fellow Superstars that make the traveling a bit more tolerable. They talk to each other freely, respect one another, and feel a special kinship because they know there is no one else who would truly be able to understand what they go through to succeed.

An Extended Family

Dean Malenko

You've got two families when you're in the wrestling industry. Your wife and kids at home and your road family. We're like a fraternity. I don't care what organization you're working for, there's a bond.

Especially when you're working overseas. When you're not sleeping, you're with the other boys—constantly. You have a special camaraderie with the guys you work with. You fight with them. You share good times, bad times, things going on back at home. Death of a family member, birth of child, you share all of this with them.

I can't count on my hands how many times I've been over in Japan and guys have found out their kids were born. Eddie Guerrero, the birth of his second daughter, is one I'll always remember. We were at a truck stop somewhere in Japan when he found out and we all shared a big bowl of spaghetti to celebrate. I know that sounds a bit odd, but that's what we did.

When we're in the dressing room or cars or sharing rooms or having a drink at the local pub one thing the guys always talk about with one another is their home life and if there's family problems or whatever. We vent to each other because we only have each other.

We all have that one common denominator, that same problem.

Nothing ever goes wrong when you're at home, things always go wrong when you're on the road and you can't do anything to fix it. The only thing you can do to keep sane is talk to your brothers on the road who understand exactly what you're going through.

Strength in numbers

Undertaker

Not everybody likes everybody. You get along with some and not others. You figure out who you are drawn to. There are some guys whose personalities match up with yours and others who don't. When you're out on the road, traveling with the same guys day in, day out, you just have to decide who falls where.

Even the ones I don't get along with great, I try to treat with respect.

There are only a few people who I let get a real inside look at me. Those are the people I can trust, that I can rely on.

I'm lucky enough to have had a few guys like that in my career. Two of my closer friends are Bryan Adams and Charles Wright [The Godfather]. I was also really close with Yokozuna. There have been a few others along the way.

We actually had a biker club type of thing. We always

took care of one another, watched one another's backs, and made sure everyone had money with them. It's easier to deal with the travel and the lifestyle when you do it in packs like that. I still keep in touch with all of those guys, even the ones not working for us anymore.

Sisterhood in the Face of Tragedy

Ivory

We had a show scheduled on September 11, 2001, in Houston. It was obviously canceled, but we all went to the building anyway. It was just everyone's natural reaction. To go to the place on the road that is your home, to be with the people who are like your family.

We spent some time there with everyone and were told to get ourselves to Nashville by Friday. With the airports shut down, I wasn't going to return the rental car I had. Molly Holly, Lilian Garcia, and I decided to drive to Tennessee together.

The three of us talked about the drive that lay ahead before we got in the car, to make sure we were all up for it emotionally. Molly suggested that with everything going on in the world, we try to make this trip as good as we could possibly make it. She remembered a fun place she once stayed in Biloxi, Mississippi, called the Beau Rivage, it was a resort and casino. We decided to drive all night and spend one wonderful day at the Beau Rivage. We were hoping it would help get our minds off of everything.

We had a system where one person would lay in the back and get some rest and the passenger was required to

talk to the driver to keep her awake. Staying up wasn't too much of challenge; we had so much to talk about that day and Lilian had her music to share when we wanted to change the subject. She would give us her new lyrics and ask us how she should sing her songs, like we know anything about it. But she listened to what we had to say. She always does.

At a bit after 2 A.M. we pulled into Biloxi. The first thing we did was get breakfast at the Waffle House across the street, then checked into the Beau Rivage about an hour later. We woke up early the next day because we wanted to get up and out of the rooms. We talked over breakfast and thought that for the first part of the day we should all deal with our 9/11 thoughts in our own way. Do what we wanted to do.

Molly went out with the car and explored the town all day. That's what she likes to do. Go see the world. She brought us back some presents—matching board shorts, Biloxi T-shirts, and those little paddleboards—saying that this was a day we could all use a toy and a new outfit.

I went for a massage and chilled out by the pool. Nothing I could do was going to take my mind off of everything and I had talked about it for hours with the girls, I wanted to do something that might help me relax a bit.

Lilian liked the idea and tried to join me out by the pool, but she just kept weeping and weeping so she talked to the front desk and they pointed out a church she could visit to attend a vigil. She went and cried her eyes out.

We met back in our rooms later in the afternoon and got ready to go out for dinner. We went to an all-you-can-eat seafood place and we shared our stories of our day and what was on our minds. We giggled and laughed and even wrestled a bit in the parking lot. It was really fun; something we needed to do.

The next morning we got up and drove right into Nashville, where Lilian's sister, Dahlia, lives and spent the day with her. Dahlia's husband was away on business so it was just us four girls. We stayed the night and the next day Molly and I got up early and went on a long jog through this rural Tennessee area. It was beautiful and relaxing.

That was a memorable trip. It was good for us to be in a car, away from the television coverage and all that. We had each other to talk to about the tragedy and could deal with it in our own way. We were traveling through a beautiful section of America, meeting wonderful people along the way. It's part of what makes this such a great country.

We were together when we needed to be but had time to decompress by ourselves when we needed that. The reason we had to make the trip was obviously tragic, but the three of us were able to pull together and form a lasting bond. For that, I am thankful.

A great Mentor

Mark Henry

Owen Hart and I traveled together when we were both in the Nation of Domination and it was one of the best times in my career. I was just coming in, making the transition and he made it easy, he taught me a lot.

He was one of the guys who didn't mind helping the other guys. This is just like any other business out there—the people who know are not always going to be generous with information on how to get better. Whether it's job security or they don't think you deserve it or they just don't like you, whatever the reason, people are not always going to help you out.

But Owen wasn't that way, man. He was just like, you know, listen to me and you'll be all right. The majority of the time we traveled together, I drove and he slept. It was his veteran's privilege. I did what I had to do.

When he was awake and we were driving along, he would talk to me about everything. How to handle the business, how to deal with people and the politics of everything—just how to be a true professional. As much as Owen was a practical joker, he was always on time. He never missed shows; he was the most reliable person you'd ever meet.

The office knew they could always trust him, even when there was stuff going on with the rest of his family. Owen was like, "That has nothing to do with me. I'll be at work on time." You could learn so much just by watching him. For him to take the time to talk to me and drive with me, spending all that time . . . it just helped me out so much.

He taught me the most of anyone I've ever known in this business.

Some Things You Can't Teach

Al Snow

Pulling ribs is a tradition that is a rich part of my experience in the business, and I try to carry it on with the younger guys like Maven and Chris [Nowinski] today. Maven is already pretty good with pulling ribs. He can keep up with me sometimes, so I have to give him some credit for that. Most people assume our history with pulling ribs on each other started on *Tough Enough,* but it didn't really. During the show we had a lot of fun with the bets and games and stuff like that, but we never got to the pranks. Because of all the other stuff we did on the show I could see the beginnings of a good prankster in him.

Right before *Tough Enough III,* I was into locking up people's stuff without them knowing. One day I went and took a few padlocks and put them on Maven's suitcase because I knew it would be a pain in the ass to open. I was impressed with how he worked his way out of this one.

He usually borrowed the rental car at night and that's

what he used to bargain with me on this one. This particular night we were at a Marriott in Atlanta that had a huge parking lot and the hotel was packed. He had a later flight the next morning and knew I had an early-morning one and would be taking the car to the airport. So he called me up when he got back to the hotel and said, "Okay, you can give me the keys to the padlocks and I'll give you the car keys."

We argued back and forth for a while, but we finally agreed to meet in the lobby and make the exchange. He passed me the car keys and I passed him off a pair of keys. The keys I gave him were fakes, of course. I go back to my room thinking I've got him.

He called me up a few minutes later and asked where the real keys were. I tried to play off like I had no idea what he's talking about. He wasn't buying that for a second. He tells me, "That's fine. I know you have an early flight so if you want to make it to the airport on time, you'll have to find your car. The car is hidden and I'm not going to tell you where it is unless you give me the real keys." I had no choice but to go and give him the real keys this time.

I gave him a lot of credit for preparing for me giving him fake keys. He was thinking ahead. He's learning from me, he's catching on to this.

The Best Travel Partner

Rey Mysterio

One of my best trips was when I had the opportunity to travel with my son when he was on vacation from school. We flew out together on a Friday-night red-eye to New York.

I did an appearance that Saturday afternoon, then house shows every night from Saturday until Tuesday.

He was on the whole loop with me, he hung on the whole way. I know he had a good time and I loved that we got a chance to be together as father and son. It was a cool experience having so much one-on-one time. You need that with your kids.

When I go home I spend most of the time with my wife and kids. But it gives me more pleasure when I can bring them on the road and spend even more time with them. With my son on that trip, for example, we got to know each other a lot more, you know, just father and son. What each is like when mom's not around. I found out that both of us can get away with a lot of things when it's just the two of us!

I don't think it hit him when he was on the road that Rey Mysterio is his dad. He's not in that mode yet, where he realizes who his dad is. I think it's actually even better this way because when kids come up and ask me for autographs when he's around he always gives me this look like he's proud of me, then says something like, "Dad, that's cool."

A Legendary Friend

A-Train

I've driven with Undertaker a few times. When I drive with guys like Test and Val [Venis] we're all talking to each other nonstop, goofing around and stuff, but when I have the chance to drive with a guy like 'Taker, I do a lot of listening.

When I'm in the car with 'Taker I don't even know how long of a trip it is, there's a smile on my face the whole time as I'm soaking it all in. He's so knowledgeable and just has so much to teach and so much to say. He's got so much information; things I never would have thought I'd need.

I've always been a fan, especially of Undertaker, so it's a cool experience. When I get the chance to ride with him, it's just amazing. Never in my wildest dreams did I think I'd be driving up and down the roads of America with Undertaker. Telling me stories, but also talking to me about personal stuff. Not confiding deep secrets or anything, just talking to me about his wife and his baby. To be on that level with him, it's unreal.

To have a bond with him where I can just say, "Hey 'Taker, how's your baby?"—it's cool. It's things like that, bonds like that, you form with the other guys when you spend hours and hours driving all over the place, that help make this job so great.

Did You Hear the One About the Five Naked Wrestlers?

Chavo Guerrero

I had a three-week tour of Japan with Chris Jericho, Jeff Farmer, and two European guys. I already knew Chris pretty well and I knew Jeff a little bit, but I never met the two Europeans. Before I left for the tour, I wasn't too excited about going over there, and it ended up being my best time ever in Japan. We all pulled together right away and formed a little fraternity. We trained together, ate together, sat on the bus together, wrestled with each other, against each other, hung out at night. The five of us were inseparable.

Now something different in Japanese hotels is they have beer in the vending machines. Right there in between the soda and water is beer. The five of us decide to get some beers while we're relaxing together in one room, and before we knew it we drank three or four floors dry. We're all feeling pretty good about now.

Then we decided to go downstairs into the hotel steam room. The Japanese are into their steam rooms, Jacuzzis, things like that, so even though we were staying at some small hotel it still had this great big steam room. On the way down, we stopped to grab some beers from a few of the floors we hadn't already wiped clean.

There we are in the steam room, drinking beer, talking about whatever came to mind when one of the guys blurts out, "Hey, you remember this song?" and started singing.

Then another guy popped out with another song. So we got five naked wrestlers sitting in a steam room singing all these songs. A bunch of Japanese guys came in wearing their towels and robes, saw what was going on and just left. We were in there for about three hours; we even started breaking it down by category . . . "Okay, let's do one-hit wonders now!"

Five naked wrestlers in a steam room, drinking beer, singing songs. Those were some good times.

The bond we all formed during this time made the trip a pleasure. Three-week tours in Japan are usually tough when you don't know a lot of the other guys going over there. You don't speak the language, you're not familiar with the food, but what a time we had.

At the end of the tour, I was ready to go home and see my family because I missed them, but I'd be lying if I didn't admit I was a little upset to be leaving those guys. Trips like that don't happen all the time.

seven

Ways to Be Entertained

"As entertainers we make our living by having people believe we are something we are not. What better way to perfect this than by never shutting that off?"

—AL SNOW

It seems that many new cars today come with a television, DVD player, Playstation 2, or some other type of entertainment device used to stave off boredom while on the road. WWE Superstars, though, rarely have that type of luxury. Standard midsize rental cars don't usually come installed with the latest home theater equipment. ✿ For the Superstar, being able to come up with creative ways to entertain themselves is about as important as mastering the full nelson. Whether it's pulling an elaborate rib (practical joke) on a fellow Superstar (or unsuspecting bystander) or putting an interesting twist on an otherwise routine activity, the men and women of the WWE have amazing ways to break up the monotony of another road trip.

They pretend to be presidents, have one another arrested, and play a lot of miniature golf.

Their imaginations have no boundaries, their senses of humor have no limits, and their quest for fun has no end.

You're in North Carolina, Now

Coach

Vince McMahon once had me arrested.

It was in September of 2000, when I was still relatively new to the company. The week before the NFL season started, Jerry Brisco asked me to run the football pool for everyone who traveled to TVs. The following Saturday, the day before the season kicked off, we were in Fayetteville, North Carolina, and Jerry caught me as we were heading into the production meeting. "Hey, Coach, you all ready?" he asked. I told him I had everything covered.

Throughout the day I was handing out the sheets for the pool and getting everybody set, it was like ten dollars to play, or something like that. This wasn't a major gambling ring.

About four-thirty that afternoon, our head of security at the time walked into the pretape room, which is where I hang out on the road, and told me he needed to speak to me out in the hallway. When I walked out there I could see he had a couple of troopers with him. I had no idea why they needed to talk to me because I knew I hadn't done anything wrong.

"We have a little problem here, Coach."

"Oh really, what's up?"

"These two men have a warrant for your arrest for illegal gambling in the state of North Carolina."

It didn't even dawn on me that the "illegal gambling" Bob was referring to could be the football sheets I handed out to everyone. "I haven't done anything. I don't know what you're talking about."

"Well, we got a report that you were selling football tickets around the arena and you gave one to an undercover cop who works with these gentlemen."

My mind started racing to think if I had given anything to anyone I didn't know. Even if I had, it was just a friendly football pool, everybody does it. As I'm standing there trying to remember everyone I gave one to, they hand me an arrest warrant.

One of the troopers then said to me, "We know you have a show tonight so we'll get you down to the precinct and back as quick as we can. Unfortunately, this is a major offense in the state of North Carolina."

The other trooper grabbed my arm and started walking with me. I couldn't believe this was happening. How was I supposed to know that picking football games with a couple of your friends was considered a major crime in North Carolina? Was I the only one who didn't study the laws of every state we traveled to?

Now we were at one end of the building and everyone—catering, all the boys, the television production people, seamstresses, you name it—they were at the other end of this one long hallway, so I knew we were going to walk past everyone to get to the big door at the back of the building.

We start down the hall and get near Vince's office. Bob told the officer in front that we had to stop and tell Vince because I'm going to be gone for a couple of hours. We knock, walk inside, and see Vince, Triple H, Stephanie McMahon, Kevin Dunn, and Jerry, who are talking about the show.

Vince stops what he's doing when he hears us and asks Bob what's going on.

"We have a little problem here. The cops arrested Coach for illegal gambling."

Calm, but as serious as he can be, Vince looks at me and asks, "What did you do?" Now I don't want to name names and sell Jerry down the river, so I just answered vaguely.

"I was asked to run a football pool for fun and apparently one of their undercover officers somehow got a copy of the sheet."

Vince walked toward me when I finished, got about four inches from my face and just went off. "A football pool? A football pool? Are you kidding me? This is the kind of shit we do not need!" I remember every other word was the f-bomb. It was the evil Mr. McMahon you see on TV multiplied by ten.

He's spitting and yelling right in my face, and to be honest, I was terrified.

He took a deep, dramatic breath and started up again. "I don't think I need to tell you the repercussions of this if it gets in the newspaper, on TV, or the Internet. If it shows up on one of those three outlets, I think you know what'll happen!"

The first thing in my head is figuring out how I'm going to tell my father I got fired for running a football pool.

The cop holding my arm spoke for the first time since we got in the office. "Excuse me, Mr. McMahon. This type of offense is usually a fifteen-hundred-dollar bond, will you be helping him with it?"

Right away he's like, "He's on his own!"

"Will you be helping him with legal representation?"

"No, he's on his own!"

I'm standing there, my heart's racing. I knew I only had thirty dollars in my wallet, and I don't know if I can use a credit card to post bail or what. By this time, Triple H, Stephanie, and Kevin have all left.

Nothing like this had ever happened to me before. It was the most terrifying experience of my life. The cops told Vince that state law required that they cuff me. Bob asked if they could at least put a towel over my hands so the cuffs wouldn't show.

Before the cop could say one way or the other, Vince answered for him. "You know, I like that idea," and he immediately started walking away from me. He went over to his bag and pulled out these dirty gym shorts and whipped them at me. They landed on my head. "Use those!"

I'm standing there, handcuffed, with a pair of Vince's dirty shorts on my head, too terrified to care. The cop took them off my head and placed them over the cuffs, then led me out of the door. And who's standing right there? Undertaker.

He looked at me and shook his head in disgust. I was humiliated. Now there's one cop in front of me, one behind me, and Vince and Brisco are about ten feet behind him. I could see the cop car outside was like thirty feet from the door, and in a spot where about three hundred fans could see me. They escorted me out there, opened the car door, and locked me in.

As they're pulling the belt on me, Vince is pacing around outside the car still screaming to no one in particular, "I can't believe this! A football pool!" He was so pissed to be bothered with this mess.

One of our security guards wanted to follow us to the station to make sure I got back as quick as possible. By this time, it's about five-fifteen and we were scheduled to start taping *SmackDown!* in a little while. We pulled out of the lot and got out to the street when the radio turns up with the other cop who stayed back at the building. This cop explained that our security guy couldn't get out, and asked if we could go back to pick him up. The cop driving is exasperated. Now, I've been instructed not to say anything, but this guy wouldn't stop talking to me as we make our way back to the building. I'm not responding to him, just pretending he wasn't there.

By the time we got back down there Vince was standing in front of everyone in the entire company who was on the road and they're all laughing their asses off. They had pulled this rib off so well.

When we got back down to the entrance and the cop who was driving the car let me out, Vince instructed him to wait a few minutes before taking the cuffs off because he thought I'd be so mad I'd start fighting somebody.

I was still cuffed but able to drop-kick his shorts at him. When I finally had the cuffs removed, I was so shaken up that I had to go to a corner of the building to calm down. I was literally trembling because I thought it was the end of my career. I was so emotional over the whole thing that I felt like I might cry and didn't really want anyone to see me break down.

To this day, Vince still calls it the greatest rib in the history of the company.

Thanks for the Lift

Al Snow

Maven, D-Von, and I were leaving a show in Halifax one night in an SUV that had running boards and a luggage rack. Now, at this building, there's one of the old security gates that they have across the garage exit. It has to be manually raised for you to get out of the building, but of course there's no one there to open it for us when we want to leave. Maven was driving and D-Von was in the backseat, so I jump out to look for someone to raise the gate—and as soon as the door shut behind me I knew I'd made a mistake.

I find the security guard, and as I'm walking back to the car I hear "click, click." They locked me out. They start to pull away, and I jump on the running board, hold on to the luggage rack, and I'm screaming at them to stop and let me in. Now Maven's driving with me hanging off the car, flopping around on the outside, and we go out the building right past all the fans who are all like, "Yeah, hey Al, how you doing?"

He keeps driving and I think, "Well, they'll stop now. They drove through all the fans, that'll be fine."

Wrong. They kept on going right out of the building, down the corner, turned at the light, down the next street. Now we've probably gone about three or four miles with me screaming on the outside of the truck when I get smart and yell, "Help! Police! Two black men are stealing my car!"

After one or two times, they finally stop the car and let me in.

A rookie of the road wars might have just panicked the whole time or jumped off right away. As a veteran of this stuff I was able take my time, relax, and figure out how to get out of the situation.

I thought to myself, "Okay, there's two black guys driving a brand-new SUV through Halifax with a white guy hanging off the luggage rack screaming. What might this look like to the police if I just yelled?"

Waiter, Please Take These Buns Away

Jerry Brisco

Back in 1979, my brother Jack and I were returning home to Tampa after a show, giving a young rookie named B. Bryan Blair a lift. Later on in his career, Bryan competed as part of the Killer Bs of the WWE.

As we were getting on to Highway 60, which is in the middle of the Florida lowlands, Pat Patterson and his friend Louie passed by us. Louie was driving, so Pat was freed up to use the moon roof for what it was really intended—he stuck his butt out and hit us with a full moon of his own.

The three of us in our car all got a big laugh out of it and started thinking about what we could do back at Pat. After tossing a couple of ideas around, Jack came up with the way.

We would put Bryan in the trunk of the car. We would slow down as we passed by Pat and hit the trunk button. Bryan would pop out of the trunk, cheeks exposed, and return the favor to Pat and Louie.

Of course, being the young guy, Bryan would do anything we asked him. We knew that there was this one truck stop on Highway 60 that Pat always stopped at because it was the last stop before Tampa. A few miles before it, we pulled over to get set up with Bryan in the trunk and all. Just as we were pulling into the truck stop, Jack and I changed our minds. We didn't chicken out; we thought of something bigger.

If we spoke loud enough, Bryan could hear us in the trunk, so we yelled to him that Pat was getting gas and would pull right by him any second. As soon as we popped the trunk, he had to jump up with the full moon.

This truck stop had a big restaurant wrapped with huge windows looking out at the parking lot. The place was packed. We told Bryan that Pat was finishing at the pump and that we'd just back up to where he was. So we started backing up, but we were actually going into a spot in front of the restaurant, right in front of the windows.

The car came to a stop, Jack hit the trunk button as we both yell, "Do it! Do it!"

Bryan sprang up immediately. Man, he was really waving his ass back and forth! Jack and I were cracking up. Bryan finally turned around and saw the full restaurant looking at his ass. He jumped out of the trunk and started pulling his pants up, stumbling around all over the parking lot.

Naturally, Jack and I did what anyone would in that situation—we took off. Before we got out of the lot, we stopped to look back at the restaurant. The whole place was hysterical laughing. Our little pit stop let Bryan pull up his pants and chase us down. He was cussing at us like heck when he got to the car. After a little more tormenting, we eventually let him back in. Jack and I had a good rib on Bryan for life.

A Few Sociological Experiments

Randy Orton

You definitely have to find some things to do when you're on the road to pass the time and take your mind off everything. Grab a decent meal, catch a movie, things like that.

I've got a bunch of things I like to do when we travel to keep entertained. If we're in a town with a mall, I like to go

Sleep where you can, when you can.

and see if anyone working there recognizes me. It's not that I'm looking for a cheap confidence boost or anything like that. I'm hoping they'll give me discounts on clothes and stuff. You'd be surprised how well it actually works. I don't pay full price for anything. Clothes, jewelry, all of it. Because they know you from TV they feel like you're one of their buddies or something and end up giving you discounts on everything.

Something else fun that Mark Jindrak and I do is to make it a point to visit strip clubs everywhere we go. When we're driving in the middle of nowhere, somewhere in the Midwest or down South, we always see these, like, one-story houses, run-down buildings, that have signs that say things like "Live Girls XXX" or "All Nude: Live Dancers."

We'll stop in there, and usually these places have food, so we'll eat and check out the strippers from these Podunk towns who usually don't have any teeth. They're all busted up in the face, not very good to look at. It's just this fascination we have.

Aside from the dancers, it's also hilarious to watch the guys who go to these strip clubs and think they're the greatest places in the world and these chicks are hot. The atmosphere in these places is so weird, it's like straight out of a movie.

Then we'll go to the best strip clubs in places like Atlanta and New York where it's completely different. We never try to pick up the girls and don't spend a ton of money, it's like our little thing where we have a good time.

It's really observational more than anything.

Make It a Light

Dr. Tom Prichard

Back in the day, me, Harvey Whippleman, Danny Davison, and Jeff Jarrett used to travel together a lot. We would drive from Memphis to the Dallas Sportatorium for a show and sometimes we would stay over and do an extra spot show in another Texas town.

There was this one time when Harvey drove Jeff's car from Memphis and met us in Dallas. He was going to drive us to the spot show on Saturday night, then drive us all back to Memphis the next day. Harvey showed up in Dallas with no gas in the car and didn't mention this to us until after the next night's show. By the time we were through with that show it was so late that we couldn't find a gas station that was open anywhere near the town we were in. We had to drive forty-five minutes out of our way to find one.

With all this going on, we wanted to get beer, too. Finally we found a gas station that could help us out on both accounts, so we filled up the car, got some beers, and were on our way back to Memphis. Harvey wanted a beer really bad but Danny wouldn't give him one because he was mad at him for forgetting to put gas in the car.

A few hours later, we made a pit stop on the side of the road. Danny drank most of his beer, but took the little he had left with him when he went to relieve himself. Somewhere along the walk, Danny decided that he would urinate into the bottle, put the cap back on, and place it back in the cooler.

We were making our way down the road for the next hour before Harvey started up again about wanting a beer. Danny finally caved and handed him a beer. You could see how happy Harvey was to have won this one. He tore the top off and took a huge swig.

"This tastes kind of salty," he said before taking a second helping. It was then that he realized he wasn't drinking beer. He tossed the bottle out the window, all pissed off, and the rest of us got a good laugh at Harvey's expense.

Red Eye Raw

Edge

After a TV taping one night in Los Angeles, Test, Christian, myself, and the two Hardys were on a red-eye back to Chicago. Everyone was going their separate ways from there.

Christian passed out within minutes of sitting down. I mean out like a light. So we got a Sharpie and some makeup from one of the stewardesses to draw on his face. His head was kind of sideways, his mouth was wide open, he was drooling . . . all the things he usually does when he sleeps. We first decided to put a People's Eyebrow on him with the Sharpie. This was when The Rock had those thick sideburns, so we drew in these big, exaggerated, fat chops on him. Then we colored the half of his face that was showing with blush, eyeliner, lipstick, whatever she had in that bag. And he didn't wake up through any of this.

Now Matt was watching all this, laughing along. But halfway through Christian's makeover Matt fell asleep, too.

What a bad move that was. I have no idea what he was thinking. He saw all of this going on, did he think we'd let him sleep in peace?

We kept it real simple with Matt, all we did was write the word "Dickhead" on his forehead. Matt woke up before Christian, so when he got up he saw the finished makeover on Christian and was cracking up.

"Oh, this is so great! We're going through O'Hare, the biggest airport in the world, and he looks like an idiot. I can't wait to land," he yelled. "We got him so good. This is awesome!"

And he was laughing like a little schoolgirl, I mean he was going nuts over the whole thing, and meanwhile he's looking at us with "Dickhead" written on his forehead. Now the rest of us were cracking up at the thought of Matt walking through O'Hare with "Dickhead" written on his forehead, but Matt thought we're only laughing at the Christian situation. We were hoping that neither of them would realize it for a while yet.

Finally, Christian started flopping at his face in his sleep and woke up. He went right into the bathroom and the rest of us were all like, "Damn, we almost had it."

When he came out, you could see his face was all scratched up, scrubbed raw, and he still had some makeup on it. Matt was still laughing at him when he got back to his seat and when the stewardess came around to bring us some drinks she looked at Matt and told him, "Oh, looks like they got you, too." Matt jumped up and took off for the bathroom. He came out with his forehead raw from scrubbing "Dickhead" off.

Sure, neither of them walked through O'Hare with the

stuff all over their face like we'd hoped, but it was still a lot of fun for the rest of us and made the time go by quickly. These are the kinds of fun things you have to do to pass the time on a red-eye flight.

Believe Us, We're Lying!

Triple H

Back when I started out with the company, we used to run two towns in the same night so the tours were much smaller.

This one night I was staying at a Sheraton in Providence, Rhode Island, with The Godwinns—Henry and Phineas—and Aldo Montoya. We went down to the bar right when we got back after the show, but the guy was closing up for the night. He turned out to be a fan, and since there were some other folks down there having a good time, he decided to keep it open for a bit. Actually, now that I think about it, I'm pretty sure I had to pay him to keep it open. Yeah, I did.

So he was making us these piña coladas with ice cream in them, not exactly "wrestler" drinks, but damn, they were good! We were really into them, just having a good time, laughing it up and all. Then Aldo ran up to his room for something. He was splitting a room with Phineas and I was sharing with Henry.

He was gone for quite a while—we thought he was maybe going to the bathroom or changing his clothes, who knew what was going on. After a little while, we all get curious, so Phineas went up to see what was going on. He came back down in about five minutes, laughing hysterically.

What happened was Phineas forgot his key, so he had to have Aldo let him in. When Aldo heard who was at the door, he thought it would be funny to be naked when he swung the door open.

So he does just that. But not only is Phineas in front of the door waiting for him, but at that same instant there was this elderly couple walking by! They look over at him, scream, and run the heck away from him. Aldo was mortified. He ducked back into the room as quick as he could to get what he needed to get. Now, as Phineas is telling us this story, we all get an idea. We had the bartender call Aldo and make like he's the manager of the hotel and there's a complaint about a naked wrestler running around the hallways causing all sorts of trouble. On a side note, I had to pay the bartender *more* money to do this. It was turning out to be an expensive night for me, but well worth it.

The bartender really played this up, saying that there is an elderly couple who just left his desk in a state of shock over the entire episode and the woman was phoning the police to file a complaint.

Aldo buys it all hook, line, and sinker.

He didn't come back down, so we all went up to the room a few minutes later. The four of us were in adjoining rooms so you could hear the conversation through the wall. As soon as Phineas walked in, Aldo started right up with what was going on.

"Yo, dude, you're never going to believe this. The manager called me just now. Those two people who were behind you in the hallway are pressing charges because they saw me naked! The cops are coming over here right now. The manager said he was gonna try to take care of it, but if he can't they're gonna need me to come downstairs and go with the cops." He was totally out of his mind. We were in the other room nearly in tears from laughing so hard. I don't know how he did it, but Phineas was playing along perfectly.

"Wow, you're kidding me? That's ridiculous!" He was saying all the right things.

Henry and I can't help ourselves, we needed to get in there. We knocked on the door, saying we'd just come up from the bar and wanted to stop in before we went to our room for the night. The first thing we asked them was if they knew what was going on downstairs because there were a bunch of cops hanging around.

"They're here for me!" yelled Aldo. He started telling us the story of what happened and, man, he is completely freaking out over it. Henry then left, saying he was heading to bed. What he did, though, was go back to our room and call the bartender. He asked him to go up to Aldo's room and pretend like he's the manager.

When the bartender identifies himself as the manager at the door, Aldo went nuts. He started running around the room, hiding beer bottles, cleaning up, anything to make it look like we weren't a bunch of drunken, rowdy wrestlers. He finally opened the door and the manager got right into it.

"Mr. Polanco"—Aldo checked in using his real last name—"look, we think we have this taken care of. The lady is really upset, though. She wants to think about it. She might press charges in the morning, but we got the police to leave for now. We do need all of your information at the front desk in the event this does become a police matter."

The "manager" left and the rest of us had to either get out of there or go to sleep or we were going to lose it and ruin the whole rib.

The next morning Henry and I told the woman at the

front desk the story and asked her to keep it rolling. When Aldo came down to check out, the woman asked for his room number, looked at the computer and said, "Oh, wow, *you're* Mr. Polanco."

Aldo was totally on edge at this point. He nearly jumped over the desk at her. "Yeah, why? What's wrong? Is something wrong?

"Well, the police were here for you again this morning."

"What? No way! I thought this was over with?"

"Sorry, sir. Actually the woman came down here early this morning and said she couldn't sleep all night because she was so disturbed, and she wanted to move ahead with the criminal charges."

That's it. Now he's totally flipped out. We convinced him to calm down and come to breakfast with the rest of us. He won't shut up the entire time.

"I can't believe this! It was a total accident and now she's going to get me in all this trouble. This is ridiculous!"

It's just hilarious how he's acting, but none of us is letting on to what's really going on. As we're sitting down, I get a page from the office (this was before we had cell phones if you can believe that!). It was from Ann in talent relations. When I called her back, I told her the whole story and asked if she would help us keep it going. She said she'd love to.

When I got back to the table I told Aldo that Ann needed him to call her right away, that's actually why she paged me. He turned white. He looked petrified.

"For what? The office never calls me. They never *need* to talk to me!"

"Sorry man, she didn't tell me what was going on, only that J.J. Dillon [the head of talent relations at the time] needs to speak with you immediately."

We finally convinced J.J. he needed to calm down for a minute and call Ann, he couldn't just ignore the office.

Ann wasted no time giving it to him.

"What did you do at the hotel last night?"

"Nothing. What do you mean?"

"Well, that's not the story we're getting. The police called J.J. early this morning to tell him that there's a woman at the Sheraton who wants to press charges against you because you were running around naked in the hallways. What do you know about that?"

He was speechless. Ann said that the police just called for J.J. and he now needs to call Aldo back in a bit, but that he shouldn't leave the hotel just yet.

He came back to the table, completely out of his mind. "I'm gonna lose my job over this! I can't believe this is happening to me!"

I mean, he's beyond upset, he is totally out of control over the whole thing. He was convinced the police were on the phone with J.J. and that J.J. was going to fire him any moment. He just wouldn't shut up about it, so in a way, it's kind of turned into a rib on us because we have to deal with this lunatic at our table losing his mind.

We tried to calm him down and shut him up, saying things like, "Dude, you have to let it go right now, there's nothing you can do." But nothing worked. He's getting worse and worse.

Finally, the three of us can't take it anymore so we cave in. We tell him the entire thing was just a rib.

But he doesn't believe us! He thought we were just trying to get him to calm down and shut up.

"No way. There's no way you guys could pull all that off, get that many people involved. You're just trying to get me to shut up about it. This is real!"

We eventually had to get most of the people involved to come over and tell him to his face that it all was a rib before he finally calmed down.

It was tremendous. One of the best ribs I've ever been a part of.

Is He Okay?

Al Snow

One of the more interesting characters I drove with back in the day was a guy named Sandy Scott. When we went into restaurants he would act like he had Tourette's Syndrome. We'd take turns doing it, but it didn't work as well when I tried because I was younger and still learning.

When he would do it, I had to keep a straight face, otherwise I'd stooge him off. It was tough not to laugh at him, but I had to play along, ask him if he took his medication, if he's feeling okay. We'd be sitting there eating and he's barking out stuff like, "Eat your popcorn, damn it!" and throwing his food all over the place. Now, he's gotta act like this and yell and scream the entire time we're there because once you start something like that you can't stop. You have to keep it up.

The different reactions you get from everyone in the place are funny. Some people just stare at you the whole

A simple little rib on Kurt Angle, Molly Holly and Trish make him employee of the month at the Evansville's Dennys.

time, some go out of their way not to look at all. And I'd just be sitting there asking him "Are you all right? Where are your pills?"

When you do things like that to entertain yourself, you're not doing it just to get a reaction or be obnoxious, but to see if you could actually pull it off. To see if you could work people and make them believe things like Sandy actually having Tourette's. As entertainers we make our living by having people believe we are something we are not. What better way to perfect this than by never shutting that off?

Who's That guy with Sergeant Slaughter?

Sergeant Slaughter

I was a bad guy, a heel, when I first came into WWE, and every place I'd go, my car would get destroyed because of it. Fans would throw a rock at it or slash the tires, something to let me know they didn't like me.

I knew I wasn't going to be able to stop them, so I looked in the newspaper for a beat-up car to drive to shows that I wouldn't mind seeing dented or anything. The first thing that caught my interest was a 1973 Cadillac Fleetwood limousine. Not only was it a different kind of vehicle, but the price was right. I called the owner and met him at his house to check it out.

It was in good shape on the outside and only had forty thousand miles on it. The guy took us out for a drive; it ran real smooth. When we got back to his place, I asked him if I had to worry about it breaking down on me.

"You don't have to worry about that with this car. We've taken great care of it."

"Yeah, well, everyone says they've taken great care of their cars," I said before the guy cut me off.

"Yeah, but we run a funeral home and this was one of our main cars. The one thing we can't afford is to have our cars break down in the middle of the funeral."

That sold me. After we got it, we took it to a military base to get it painted camouflage. The camouflage paint sure made it look neat, but it also made it a traveling bull's-eye. It was terrible what they did with that car. The fans just beat it to death. We had the military lead paint on there the first time, it was real easy to scratch, so what a lot of people would do was carve their names or swear words on it. We had some pretty bad stuff on there if I remember right. There was also this one huge heart that someone drew on the roof that said "Mary Loves John." That one wasn't exactly the toughest decoration for a mean wrestler to have on his car.

It certainly wasn't all bad, though. We could have some fun with that car. This one time, we were driving up from Philadelphia during a holiday weekend in the summer— Memorial Day, Labor Day, the Fourth of July, one of those. Somewhere on the New Jersey Turnpike, we came up on this long army convoy with dozens of military vehicles one after the next. As we were passing it all the soldiers are honking their horns yelling "USA, USA!" This was at a time when I was a good guy.

When we got to the end of the convoy, we pulled up alongside the jeep that was leading and the guys looked over at us and gave us a smile. I told my driver to pull up in front of them and lead the convoy. They were all going nuts when he pulled up. Honking their horns, chanting even louder now. "USA! USA! USA!"

So we look like we're leading this thing when we roll up to the next toll booth. My driver put down his window at the booth and explained to the teller, "Official government business here. We have President Reagan in the back. Please don't tell anyone or make a scene. It's official government business. We have President Reagan and Sgt. Slaughter in the back of this vehicle, but don't say anything."

She didn't listen to him for nothing. She yelled out, "Oh my God! President Reagan and Sgt. Slaughter are in that car!"

My driver said, "I told you not to say anything!" and took right off. We didn't get very far before the police started chasing us and pulled us over. Turned out they really thought we had President Reagan in our car, so they wanted to stop us to see for themselves. We had to come clean and tell them that President Reagan wasn't really in the car, but Sgt. Slaughter was.

They had a great sense of humor and laughed about the whole thing. I signed some autographs for them and everyone got on their way.

I've always thought those cops really just wanted to meet me but had to say President Reagan's name to make it seem like more of a legitimate traffic stop.

The Good Old Windmill

A-Train

A couple of us guys have a running miniature golf tournament. When we have a few hours off we try to find a miniature golf course near the building and get out there. It's a good way to relax and get your mind off everything else, we always have such a good time when we play. The visual alone is hilarious.

Families playing with a bunch of kids, then you got me, Bradshaw, the Bashams, Rey Mysterio, we all get out there. So many different sizes, shapes, a guy with tons of piercings, a little guy we make play with his mask on sometimes. It's great.

The set up of the tournament is teams; you play with the same partner and after a couple of rounds we have a tournament winner then start over. I play with Jimmy Korderas, the referee, and we're the best.

Something happened to Jimmy and I through the summer of 2003, though. We hit a rough patch. Our play was off for a few rounds. It got so bad, we actually lost the championship for a while to ring announcer Tony Chimel and referee Brian Hebner. We figured out what was wrong, though, and got back on track. Tony and Brian are tough. You gotta be on top of your game to take them down.

Bradshaw and his partner, the trainer Larry Hecht, are consistently in the top three, too. They're a solid team; don't have many bad rounds. You'd never guess that there are a lot of talented mini-golfers in the locker room. The competition is always tough.

For me, my regular golf game helps me out on the miniature course. My short game is great, it's the long game I'm terrible at. That's what kills me when I'm out on the real course. When it comes to putting and especially gimmick putting, I can more than hold my own. Hitting the iron corners, getting up the loop-the-loop, the windmill. I'm on it.

Gotta love the windmill. Not only the best miniature golf gimmick, but I kissed my first girl behind a windmill on a miniature golf course.

I love the windmill.

A Complete 180

Rey Mysterio

On one of our European tours, I passed out on the plane ride home and some of the guys messed with me. They drew on my face, took pictures of me holding stupid signs they made up. Stuff like that. Nothing crazy, just little things for a laugh.

After that trip I decided I'm not going to sleep on anymore flights with all the boys.

A few months later we were doing another international tour. This one went to Russia, then Osaka, Japan, and finally Thailand. When we were on the way back home, everyone is trying to have fun, you know, celebrating because this long tour is over. Some people are having a drink, some people are reading a book, whatever they enjoy.

But there comes a time on all these flights when everyone starts passing out one by one. With my new promise to stay awake on all plane rides, I decided that I was going to mess around with some of the guys the way they did to me when I fell asleep.

Charlie Haas, who was passed out right in front of me, was going to be my first victim.

I called over Nidia and told her to bring her camera. We started out small by sticking paper up his nose and taking pictures of that. When we realized he wasn't moving, that he was too deeply asleep, we started getting more and more creative.

We had Nidia sitting next to him doing some funny stuff. Then I got into it. So we're both surrounding him, with the paper in his nose, having someone else take pictures—all sorts of stuff.

About two weeks later we're at TV's and we called him over. We told him Nidia got her pictures back from Thailand, he should take a look at them. And his pictures are mixed right in there.

Charlie was a good sport, he thought it was kind of funny that we could do all this around him and he didn't wake up.

Now that I have this "no sleep" policy and I'm the guy who messes with people rather than the other way around, I'm really looking forward to our next international tour. I've got some big plans.

Hit the Snooze Button on This Thing

Al Snow

Early on in my career I rode with the guy who trained me, Jim Lancaster. I always had to be on my toes for pranks with him. I think that's why I'm able to pull them off now. You just never knew when he was going to do something, and he was a quick-thinker.

One time he wanted to emphasize the "Don't fall asleep in the car" rule, which you never do because you're at the mercy of the person driving the car. Well, we're on a long drive home to Ohio, back from St. Louis. During the drives, we used to sit there and talk for hours and book territories. I learned so much just sitting in the car with him.

Well, this one time I started falling asleep and the next thing I know I hear this noise—*Wham!*—and the car swerves.

It wakes me up right away and Jim starts getting upset. I look in the rearview mirror and see that there's a car on the side of the road behind us, right where we swerved. I didn't see anything else, just the emergency flashers.

And Jim says, "Oh my God. I hit somebody, I hit somebody!" I asked him if he hit the car, but he said, "No, no, I hit a person. They were standing alongside the car." He was so convincing. For the next two hours he kept it up and had me believing that we actually struck somebody, had hit a human being. I am all scared and panicked, pleading with him to go back and explain to the cops that he didn't see anyone standing there. He's absolutely refusing, "No way. I gotta just keep driving. We can't go back now."

After he had his fun for a few hours he finally told me that all he did was slam his hand against the dashboard and swerve the car. There was never anyone near the car, it was just abandoned on the side of the road and he thought it would be a funny way to teach me a lesson. But that's how fast he could come up with ideas to get you. He saw that car and thought of this whole thing right away. And I'll tell you, I never fell asleep in his car again.

Can I Borrow Your Tumor?

Chris Nowinski

I had a benign tumor. It started as a little lump, then just kept getting bigger and eventually started to hurt. When they removed it, I asked to keep it because I wanted to see what it looked like.

After the surgery they gave it to me in a jar of formaldehyde with a screw-off lid. When I was telling the guys in the locker room about the surgery before I went in, a bunch of them asked me to bring the tumor back with me. Well, it just so happened that we had a *SmackDown!* in Manchester right after I went through the procedure, so I drove out to Boston and stuck the tumor in the car.

When I got backstage I was just carrying it around with me, like it was a pet or something. All the boys who saw it thought it was one of the coolest things in the world.

Except for Jerry Brisco.

I didn't know that he had such a weak stomach. He asked what I was holding on to when he walked by me and as soon as he saw it he started gagging. He threatened bodily harm if I brought it any closer to him. This little jar turned him into a mess.

Shane McMahon caught that exchange and decided to push the envelope a little bit with Jerry. Shane and Bruce decided to borrow my tumor to play some jokes on Jerry. They waited until the show actually started so Jerry would be locked in the gorilla position, backstage, stuck behind a table.

At first they were not very creative. They just took it and both walked up giggling and shoved it in his face. Jerry jumped back against the wall screaming, "If you bring that any closer, I will kill you both!"

They had their good laugh and they got out of there.

But then the wheels started turning a little more for them. They walked over to catering and found an empty jar that looked similar to the one that held my tumor. Then they filled it with liquid and dropped a chunk of meat in there. From far away it looked so much like the actual tumor. What a brilliant idea!

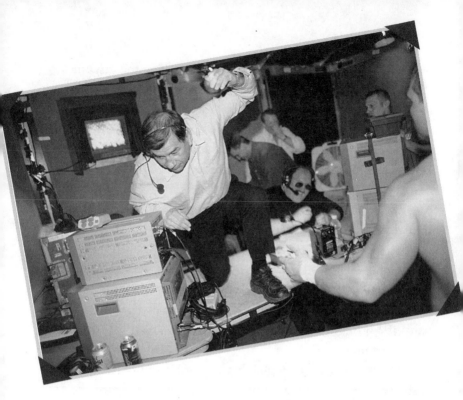

The two of them snuck up the stairs. Keep in mind, this was all happening while a *Raw* match was going on. Live television right outside the curtain from where Jerry sat.

They walked right up to the table and threw the contents of the cup onto Jerry so he thought he got hit by my tumor. He pulled off this Superman-like leap, going from a sitting position to actually clear the table with one jump. He ran for the door, but it was locked. Then he made a mad dash for the stage just to get out of the area. Halfway through the curtain he realized there was a live television show going on on the other side, so he stopped himself.

Jerry refused to get back behind his desk until they cleaned it off and told him it wasn't actually the tumor.

He totally flipped out over the whole thing. Even

though he found out that it wasn't a real tumor, he still couldn't calm down. He wasn't the same guy for the rest of the night.

It's Not Poisonous

D-Von Dudley

Back around the time we had our first Pay-Per-View in ECW, business was really picking up. The paychecks were getting bigger and we were starting to travel away from the Northeast to do shows.

One of the places we were booked was Louisiana. Most of the boys were thrilled to go, but the minute I found out about this trip, I was nervous. You see, I'm afraid of snakes. I absolutely hate them. Anybody from New York City or anywhere in the upper eastern part of the country usually doesn't like snakes because they're not used to seeing them. And I hate them.

The show was in Baton Rouge and we were staying in New Orleans. When we pulled up to the hotel, I was watching every single step I took walking out of the car because I was petrified I was going to see snakes everywhere I went. I was thinking in Louisiana there's swamps and bayous all over the place, so that meant the snakes lived everywhere. I had to stay alert.

Pretty much the whole locker room knew I was afraid of snakes and was nervous about this trip because it was all I talked about for weeks. So, of course, the guys I was traveling with came up with a rib to pull on me while we were there.

One of the guys, Sign Guy Dudley, bought this rubber

snake before we left. Another guy, Jack Victory, one of the old-timers, was riding with us as well. The two of them had a plan; they were going to spring it on me once we were in the room.

Even though the paychecks were getting bigger, we were all a close-knit family and trying to save money, so the three of us were sharing a room on this trip.

The first night we're there, a bunch of us were planning to go out on Bourbon Street together. I was the first one ready and was playing a Playstation baseball game while I was waiting on everyone else. Sign Guy is getting dressed and asked me to do him a favor and go out on the terrace to see if it was raining.

I pulled back the curtain, tried to slide the door open, but it wasn't going anywhere. There was one of those blockers, like a wooden stick, holding it back. So I went to pull it out and as I looked down I see this snake. I jumped up screaming and ran clear across the room.

"This is it! There's a snake over there! I can't take it! This is it! I'm calling Paul E. [Heyman] and telling him I can't do this anymore. I'm going to tell Paul E. I don't care about anything, I can't work the South no more!"

I ran to the phone to call the front desk to tell someone to come get this thing out of our room. I couldn't even dial the phone I was so frantic. My hands were shaking. Sign Guy and Jack are laughing uncontrollably and I scream at them, "What's so funny? There's a snake over there!"

I just dropped the phone, grabbed my bag, and started throwing stuff in there to pack. Sign Guy goes over, picks up the snake, and walks over to me. I took a swing at him. As he jumped back to avoid my fist, he let go of the snake and it fell to the carpet. That's when I saw it was a fake, rubber snake.

They were laughing at me for days. They still call me up and rib me about it to this day. To think, I was going to walk out on the tour and never again work in the South, all over a rubber snake.

eight

Back in the Day

*"Hey man, here's a hundred dollars Canadian,
you're going to Japan, hopefully someone will be at
the airport to pick you up. See you in three weeks."
—CHRIS JERICHO

Most WWE Superstars didn't just show up one day in the big-time, ready to hop on the charter flight over to Europe where a company bus would drive them around. There are some that did, but the majority of them had to build up to their dream of becoming a Superstar, taking whatever jobs came their way. ✪ Driving hundreds of miles to perform for a dozen fans and twenty bucks was not unusual for most of the men and women on the current WWE roster. They endured these early hardships, hoping that one day it would lead to their ultimate goal.

You might think the Superstars who took this route would be jealous of the ones who arrived on the scene in a limousine, but the opposite is true; they have sympathy for them. Sad that these Superstars will never experience the complete journey from the bottom to the top of the business. A journey that, although extremely difficult at times, yielded some of their most cherished memories.

The Bermuda Triangle of Decadence

Chris Jericho

One of the guys I was wrestling with in Mexico a while back told me about this tournament they held in Hamburg, Germany. It would last for six weeks and every night would be in the same building, you'd just go there and wrestle every night in the same place.

So I wrote a letter to the promoter and included a couple of pictures. I told him I would love to come to Germany to wrestle in this tournament. I thought it would be great experience and a lot of fun, just another place to visit. At the time, I was interested in going to as many places as I could, in having as many experiences as I could.

My career was really hot in Mexico, but I wanted somewhere else to go. I figured, what the hell, I'll go to Germany for six weeks, it'll be fun.

A few weeks after I sent out the letter, the promoter wrote back and said he'd love to have me, here are the dates. I wrote back asking if I get a plane ticket, a visa, anything. He wrote back again saying that we are responsible for our own plane tickets, and told me how much money we make. I think it was eighty deutschmarks a day or something like that. He told me I didn't need a visa, just say I was coming as a tourist.

The wrestler who told me about the tournament also mentioned that I should be sure to ask the promoter to get me a reservation at the Hotel Damshank, that's the place where all the boys stay.

In one of the promoter's letters he mentioned that he made the reservation and he'd pick me up at the airport. That night I made my travel plans and wrote him one final time to pass along my flight information. Now, this is all by handwritten letters, no phone calls, no e-mail. This is literally the U.S. Postal Service, or actually the Mexican post office.

When I landed in Germany I noticed there were no customs agents. I just walked right through. I could have been carrying a thousand dollars of weed in my bag, no one would have known. My flight was late by like twenty minutes, and when I got to the lobby, there's no guy waiting for me. I stayed for a while, but no one showed up.

I jumped in a cab and gave the driver the address for the Hotel Damshank, it was all I had. I was going to Germany for six weeks and the only things I was carrying was one guy's name, one address, and a plane ticket for a return flight in six weeks that couldn't be changed because I bought it so cheap.

When I finally got to the hotel, I asked the clerk for my reservation. I could tell right away that this wasn't the nicest guy in the world just by the face he made when I spoke.

"You have no reservation here."

I told him I was certain I did, there must be some mistake, could he please check again.

"You have no reservation here, we are full. You go. Go away."

Talking to this guy was hopeless. I asked if he knew of any wrestling around the area and he points out the window, toward this field where I see a tent. It looked like a toy, that's how far away it was. I have these two hockey bags filled with three weeks' worth of clothes—so I only had to do laundry once—a ghetto blaster, and all my music.

I start walking the distance of about two or three football fields to get to the tent. I go inside and there are a few guys sweeping the floor. I asked them if they knew where Renee was, I tried to pronounce his last name but of course I was saying it wrong and they're all like, "Who? Who?"

Finally, this old Swiss guy comes up to me and says, "Yeah, I waited for your flight but it didn't show up so I left."

"It showed up twenty minutes late."

"Well sorry, I left. I'm glad you found your way."

"I'm having a problem with my room over at the Damshank, can you come help me out?"

"Oh sorry, you don't have a reservation. It was full."

"Okay, well, do you have a reservation for me anywhere?"

"No."

"Well, what the hell do I do now?"

"I'll take you down to the Reeperbahn and we'll look there."

I had no clue at the time, but the Reeperbahn is the red-light district, like an Amsterdam-type place. All there is in the Reeperbahn are strip clubs, music shops, bars, and sex shops. I'm walking up and down the Reeperbahn with these two huge hockey bags asking how much it costs to stay in these motels.

I'm making like eighty deutschmarks a night and all these motels are like seventy. I'd only have ten deutschmarks to eat, so I can't do it. Finally I found this place called the Hotel Rheinland or something like that and they'd give me a room for thirty deutschmarks a night. Now this motel had a McDonald's to the left, a strip club to the right, and an old concert hall across the street. It was the Bermuda Triangle of decadence and I was right in the middle of it.

The next day I went back to the tent, met a few of the guys. Two of them were from Liverpool and we went back to their hotel to hang out and grab something to eat. They were staying at another place in the Reeperbahn and I remember they had a bloodstain on their wall and I told them, "At least my hotel isn't as bad as yours."

Back at the Hotel Rheinland, it took me three weeks to figure out how to lock the door. I thought it had been locked the whole time I was there, then one day some German guy just walks into my room as I was reading and started talking to me in German. I started screaming, "Get out, get out!

I had to get up and physically throw him out of the room. I looked at the door and only then realized you had to lock the door from the inside with a key like an old-school Alfred Hitchcock movie.

This place was just like all the other motels in Europe where you only have one bathroom on a floor, kind of like your house. So you're sharing the toilet with people who are staying in the six other rooms. After a while you just end up pissing in the sink because you can't hold it any longer waiting for everyone else to finish up.

I think by the time I made my money on the tour I ended up breaking even or something along those lines. It may have even cost me money to go between the plane ticket, the hotel, and food.

Looking back it was one of the best experiences of my life.

Is Every Trip Like This?

Dr. Tom Prichard

I was still working as a promoter's assistant when I had my first wrestling match. My first official road trip was from Houston to Shreveport. We left Houston late at night, after the show, so we could spend the night and wake up in Shreveport.

Because I had no idea where I was going, I followed Boyd Pierce, the announcer, the whole trip. We were moving along in the left lane when in my rearview mirror I noticed a car hauling ass behind me.

Both Boyd and I moved over to the right lane to let this maniac on through. This guy was totally out of control. Then, for no reason at all, he moves over and starts driving on the shoulder. And he's going faster. Something had to be going on with this guy.

He stays on the shoulder and before he can get back on the actual road, he hits a ramp and totally flips the car over. An instant later, the car fell over the side of the freeway.

I think both Boyd and I were in shock. We both just kept on driving. One of the things that really freaked me out was that as soon as that car went over the freeway, the

AC/DC song "Highway to Hell" came on the radio. I swear this is true. I'll never forget that.

Boyd wanted me to come along with him to breakfast the next morning where he was meeting one of his friends, a fellow wrestler. This was the first time I ever met Michael Hayes. Over the years I'd come to have a lot of great memories from the road with Michael, and this was a great way to start it off.

Feels Like the First Time

John Cena

My first trip to do a show was while I was training in Southern California. The show was for an independent outfit and was at an out-of-the-way place called The Coach House. Now, I'd never done a show or anything like this before. I mean, I'd had a few practices, but no matches in front of an audience.

Man, I remember we must have driven almost four hours to get to this bar and I had a piece of crap for a car back then. It was a '91 Continental with no driver's side mirror, no air-conditioning, nothing like that. It was a struggle just to get to the place, but it ended up being a real good deal.

When we walked in there were maybe twenty-five people in the crowd. But I thought it was the greatest thing in the world to go out in front of these people to show them what I got and try to entertain them. The job didn't even pay anything, but that didn't matter either. You do this because you love it. You just love to be in that ring entertaining people. That's the only thing that matters.

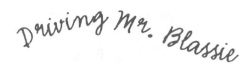

Driving Mr. Blassie

Paul Heyman

Freddie Blassie was one of the funniest, most colorful people you could ever meet. He loved the wrestling business with a passion few could ever rival. His profanity-laced tirades were done with such outrageousness that even the victim of the tongue-lashing usually admired the style with which Blassie cut them down. The one thing Freddie couldn't do well, though, was drive. In fact, he was the worst driver on the planet.

Freddie lived in Hartsdale, New York, just about ten minutes from my parents' house in Scarsdale. Back in the early eighties, Blassie would meet everyone at the monthly Madison Square Garden shows promoted by Vince J. McMahon (father of present WWE chairman Vincent Kennedy McMahon), and then travel for two days of television tapings in Allentown, Pennsylvania (the flagship "Championship Wrestling"), and Hamburg, Pennsylvania ("All Star Wrestling").

But on one particular night at the Garden, Blassie had forgotten to pack the new sequined jacket he had wanted to wear on television. And boy, did he let everyone know how pissed he was when he realized the jacket wasn't in his suitcase.

I was taking pictures in the locker room for one of the newsstand wrestling magazines when Freddie started yelling at me. "Hey kid, don't you live in Scarsdale?"

Uh oh. Somehow, this was all going to be my fault. "Um, yes sir, I do. . . ."

Blassie's face got all red. "Don't 'yes sir' me, kid, just tell me if you live there!" I nodded my head in the affirmative. Blassie was about to tear into me, or so I thought. "How do you get home from the Garden?" he asked.

"Well, after the show," I responded, "I usually take the train."

Lou Albano always jokingly told Freddie that I wasn't really a high school student, but a college kid who pretended to be younger (which, in Lou's inebriated state, was probably something the Captain really believed). Blassie started yelling about how he had to go home and get his jacket, and *then* in the morning go to Allentown, about a hundred-mile drive.

"You're not taking the train home tonight!" Blassie yelled so everyone within earshot could hear him. "You're going with me!"

After the Garden show, Freddie and I hopped in a cab over to the Ramada Inn in Manhattan where almost everyone used to stay. Blassie parked his car there, because he didn't want the throngs outside MSG to know which car was his. So after insulting a few dozen people at the parking garage (and—once again—making even the victims love every moment of the experience), Blassie and I embarked on our thirty-minute journey from Midtown Manhattan to Westchester County.

There's something you need to know. In "old school" tradition, you never let the person pulling a practical joke on you know you're sweating the gag. Whether it's a simple rib or an elaborate scheme, the worst thing you can do is let the person "getting you" know you're "getting got."

So Blassie peels out of the Ramada parking garage and

decides we should take the FDR Drive, which runs along the east side of Manhattan. "All the bad drivers take the West Side Highway," he said. Freddie was yelling at all the other drivers as he sped through the streets of Manhattan, including screaming at a cabdriver who had to slam on his brakes to avoid hitting us as we ran the red light at Sixty-second and Lexington. "Those taxis should all be banned in the summer time," Freddie professed. "If people walked, they'd get better tans anyway!"

I was starting to get nervous. I couldn't let Freddie know, though. Never let 'em know they're getting to you. This had to be a joke. He can't be *this* much of a maniac behind the wheel.

Freddie swerved onto the FDR Drive at Sixty-second Street, and immediately wandered into the middle lane for no rhyme or reason, cutting off a Chevy Nova in the process. My heart was pounding. I mean, *that* was close. I glanced over, and Freddie looked like he didn't even notice we almost had a wreck. He was looking for his cassette tape of the Platters. Aw, he knew we cut that person off. I mean, we damn near wiped out. He *had* to know . . . didn't he?

The erratic driving continued as Freddie picked up the Deegan Expressway going north to Westchester. It was getting hard not to admit absolute fear. Freddie was trying to find "Only You" on the tape, screaming at the tape itself, as people were honking their horns and giving Freddie the finger from both the left lane (which we would drift into) and the right lane (same story, different lane). "They all hate me!" Freddie mentioned to me, as if to let me know he noticed the scene he was causing as we meandered into the left lane as we passed Yankee Stadium. "That's the art of being a heel!"

I was dripping with sweat. Blassie was going to kill us. "Freddie," I started to say, "um, aren't we kinda . . ." *Bam!* Freddie slammed the front driver's side tire onto the divider that separates northbound traffic from southbound traffic. The rear wheel followed. This was like an amusement park ride. We were driving northbound, with two wheels on the divider, and two on the shoulder. I couldn't take it anymore! I had to scream.

"Stop the car!" I finally exclaimed. *"Pull the f over!"*

Bad-oom-boom! Freddie cut the steering wheel all the way right, bringing the left side of the car down off the divider, and cutting across all three lanes of the Deegan, finally coming to a halt on the right-side shoulder. "Jeez, kid, you're going to give me a heart attack!" Blassie said. "What's the matter? You gotta pee or something?"

This was just too much. "Are you kidding?" I gasped. "You're going to kill us both! You've cut everyone off, you've gone from one lane to the other, and back again!" I was in tears. I was scared for my life.

Blassie started to laugh. "I have eighty percent vision in one eye," Freddie said, "and probably twenty percent vision in the other. Together, they make one good eye."

All the cars we had cut off were flying past us now, honking their horns, throwing things at us. Freddie hollered back, "Ya bunch of pencil neck geeks" and other assorted insults. Freddie jumped out of the car. Oh my God. He was going to attack someone. Freddie ripped open my door. "Slide over, you're driving!"

This was a welcome sign that Freddie realized his erratic driving was a hazard to the residents of the state of New York, except for the fact that I, the appointed driver at

1 A.M., had never driven a car before! Do I mention this to Freddie? If I do he'll take the wheel again. So I shut up and put the gear shift in Drive.

As bad as my first-time driving must have been, it couldn't have been nearly as dangerous as Blassie's lethal automotive operational skills.

I followed Freddie's instructions back to his house, where he invited me in. I called my father, who was wondering why I was so late, since I had school the next morning. My dad, a lawyer of many years in New York, came to pick me up. Freddie told my father about leaving the sequined jacket home, how he had to drive to Allentown in the morning, the whole story. My father was laughing his ass off. "Well, I hope you guys had a fun ride home!" he said as the evening was drawing to a close.

As I hopped into my dad's car, Freddie said to me, "I thought Albano was telling me the truth! I didn't know you're really a high school kid!" Then he looked at my dad and told him, "It's really a pleasure to meet you. Paul is ambitious, hardworking, and is a real go-getter." My father was so proud to hear this.

"Just one thing," Freddie said, as he shook my dad's hand. "Your son is the worst driver I've ever been with in my entire life!"

Thrifty Travel Tips

Jim "J.R." Ross

When I started out in the business, I wasn't really making any money. You're talking somewhere between forty and sixty bucks for a full night of refereeing the whole card. Maybe you'd get an extra five if you took a big bump or something, but for the most part it averaged out to about fifty a night. Because of this, I learned some great ways to save and stretch my money while on the road.

FOOD

When it came to eating there was only one word I needed to know: buffet. It was important to know where all the buffets were along your usual driving route and what time your favorite ones closed. Now, the big trick with the buffet is you wanted to eat in the late afternoon, like three or four, so that you could get away without having to eat a big supper. Everything after breakfast just kind of converged into one huge meal at the buffet. The Chinese buffets were the coolest things in the world. They would cost you only about $2.99 and were usually open real late. They'd fill you up and not empty out your pockets.

TRANSPORTATION

We drove everywhere in our own cars. And we were responsible for all the expenses: our own gasoline, hotel rooms, food. There were no reimbursements from the office.

What we'd do to save money was pack three and four in someone's car and all the passengers paid the driver two cents a mile. That was the agreed upon rate in the locker room. It doesn't sound like much now, but we needed everything we could get then. If you put three guys in your car for a two-hundred-mile trip, you made twelve bucks between them. That would pay your gas.

And think of it this way, if you had guys paying you twelve in trans fees and your payoff that night for refereeing was fifty, that twelve bucks was a significant percentage of your full pay for the night.

The two cents a mile was a good deal, but I actually worked an even better one for a while.

There was one main-event guy who had what I'll call a healthy libido. He was married but had lots of girlfriends everywhere and got laid a lot on the road. He would pay me a nickel a mile, more than double the usual rate, for taking him to his local girlfriend's house after a show and wait for him to do his thing. This nickel a mile covered a large part of my expenses. I figured I could afford to take a nap in my car while he was taking care of business in the house.

HOTELS

You always shared a room and didn't always get a bed. Only two guys would go check in and then the other two would sneak in to keep the cost down. That meant there were no cots or roll-away beds because the front desk thought you only had two guys in there. So with two beds for four guys, the senior guys got beds, the younger guys got the floor. I was always one of the younger guys.

Another great trick was the hotel two-for-one. What you'd do is find a hotel in the next town that was sympathetic to your cause, drive all night to get there, and check in at sunrise. Theoretically, in your mind, you were getting an extra day.

You were checking in at like six or seven one morning and wouldn't have to check out until the next afternoon, like thirty-six hours later. If you went to sleep right when you got there, then slept again after that night's show, it was like you were getting two nights sleep but only had to pay one.

part of the Journey

Edge

Growing up in the business in Canada, I had so many insane trips. Trips where if it was in the winter we drove across frozen lakes, or if it was the summer, we took four-seater pontoon planes and landed on the same lakes we usually drove across. I've had to drive for hours through parts of Canada with no signs of any real civilization.

There are a million times, but some of them stick out for me. This one time we were in a van with like half a dozen or so guys and it broke down. We all got out to see what the deal was and this other van came driving by and offered to help us, but this one could only fit two guys.

It had these gas tanks in the back where they could fit the two people who could sit on them. Somehow, Christian and I got voted to go in the van and ride to the next town. Well, the next town was four hours away and they're these winter roads, so it's not even regular roads. We sat on the gas tanks and got a total contact high from inhaling all the fumes. It was just a brutal trip. When we finally get to the next town, we're freezing cold and light-headed—and we had to find someone to go right back to where the other guys were stranded to fix the van. It was just one of those nights.

There was another night where we got chased off a reservation by cars of Indians with hockey sticks. I still don't know what happened, maybe it was a mix up with the promoting deal where someone didn't get their money or whatever. All I know is a bunch of us are in the back talking and all of sudden someone yelled to us to run to the truck right away. We all took off and good thing we did. A bunch of the natives from the reservation where we did the show were coming after us swinging hockey sticks. It also could have been that someone had gotten too much heat in the ring and it just carried over a bit too far, I don't know. We had to go as fast as we could on those roads, which wasn't too fast, but we did make it off the reservation and away from them.

Back when all of this stuff was going on, I never got depressed about thinking the rest of my life was going to be one insane road trip after another. Deep down I always told myself I was going to make it to where I am now. That was never a doubt. It wasn't cockiness, but confidence, which I thought I was going to need to make it to the WWE.

I knew that these trips were all a test for me to pass and get the experience I needed for where I wanted to get to. I just kind of looked at it as a set of challenges that would lead me to my dream. That's why I could keep a good sense of humor while it was happening.

I knew these stories would be the kind that I'd be able to look back on, even in thirty years, and laugh about.

If I looked at it any differently, I would have given up. I was wrestling in front of twenty Indian kids, sleeping on blue mats in a gymnasium, and making Kraft macaroni and cheese dinners in the home economics room. If I had sat back and asked myself, "Am I going to do this for twenty years?" I'd be so depressed I'd probably would have quit.

You Want Me to Park This?

Booker T

I was at one of my first really big autograph signings at the Compaq Center, appearing for a group that I was in at the time called the Western Wrestling Alumni, the WWA. When I drove up to the building I was in my old Thunder-

Booker T still has the car he promised himself, and it's in mint condition.

bird, it was like a 1979 I think, real old. All the tires were all beat up. I didn't even have the inspection sticker on it or anything like that.

I pulled up to the place and circled around a couple of times looking for where I was supposed to park. I couldn't find anything so I drove up to the very front of the building to run into the box office and ask. As I made my way over I saw a cop talking to some fans.

I told him I was there to do an autograph session with the WWA and had no idea where to park. He said, "Oh, you're one of the wrestlers. You're a celebrity so they'll park your car for you." I was really kind of embarrassed at this. I didn't exactly have the best-looking ride out there. It definitely did not need a valet and all this special attention.

Eventually I gave in and let them park it. I was still a bit embarrassed about the whole thing. After the show I vowed to myself that I'd never go to another autograph signing with a car looking like that.

Reaching the Stars

Chavo Guerrero

The first time I had to take a plane to get to a show was a big deal for me. I was so excited.

I couldn't believe that someone would actually pay to fly me somewhere to wrestle. I was amazed that someone thought enough of my ability to spend money on a plane ticket. I remember thinking to myself as I boarded the plane, "I made it."

Even though it was just for a little indy show, I truly felt like I made it. I watched my dad wrestling for years and now here I was, following him. Growing up, Eddie [Guerrero] and I dreamed about it. We never wanted to be anything but wrestlers. We had a ring in the backyard and we were inside it all the time; it was all we talked about and this trip made me feel like I was really doing it. I'd achieved my lifelong dream.

I was on cloud nine in that plane, feeling like a big shot, like I'd made it.

The funny thing about the trip is that I was feeling so good about the actual trip, but when I got to the show and worked, I was horrible. I can't even remember what city it was in, I know it was somewhere in North Carolina in front of maybe a hundred people, but I don't know which town or who I even wrestled that night. I think over the years I forgot that stuff because I was so bad that night, but the experience as a whole was one I'll never forget.

Always an Adventure

Booker T

It's funny to think about how we've gone up and down the road. We've driven eight hundred miles for a $125 payoff. We've gone three hundred miles in horrible weather all to collect $25 at the end of the night.

But you know, those are some of my fondest memories of my days in the business. Coming up in the business is a struggle for most people. For me, traveling all over the country, no matter what the conditions or what the payoff was, it was always like an adventure. To get out there and see it all.

It was almost like being a Boy Scout, being able to go out in the wilderness and just have fun, never knowing what you're going to find.

Coming from my neighborhood, these adventures were nothing I ever imagined doing, so the travel was something I always looked forward to. I was just having fun doing it, never even thinking about the money.

When I got to the big time it became a business. The fun was definitely still there and so were the fans, but just the joy of that adventure, that's what changed a little bit.

Of Hotcakes, One Hundred Dollars, and Dreams

Chris Jericho

Going to Japan was always one of my dreams. I mean, who wouldn't want to go to Japan? I was twenty years old my first time, to go there to wrestle and get paid for it? I didn't get paid much, but I didn't care. At that time to get to go to Japan to wrestle was the cat's ass.

I was with a small company called FFW the first time I went and didn't even have a work visa. I was told to just write down one of the Japanese wrestler's addresses and say I was staying at his house for a visit, and if the authorities saw my wrestling gear and started asking questions, tell them I might have a tryout or something.

It took fifteen hours to fly directly from Calgary to Tokyo. I got off the plane, rounded up my bags, and man, that's it. I didn't know what I was doing. I had no visa, no addresses, no money. I mean, I had one hundred Canadian dollars, but that's it. Luckily, someone from the promotion was there to pick me up because if they didn't show, man, I was screwed.

You really develop a sense of independence when you first start traveling overseas because there's such an unknown factor, such an X factor. You don't know what to expect, you don't have a clue what's coming up.

The whole first time I was there all I ate were pancakes, Kentucky Fried Chicken, and McDonald's; they were the only things I saw there that were familiar. I used to drink a lot of milk back then, too, and this one day I bought a gallon, downed half of it in one gulp, and threw up right away because I didn't realize it was soy milk and it smelled and tasted like piss. These are the kinds of things you don't really know until you're there.

Another day I was trying to order pancakes, which are called hotcakes over there. I looked at the guy and said, "Hotcakes." He glared back at me like this was the first time he ever heard anything that sounded remotely close to that word. I repeated it, "Hotcakes." Still nothing. Finally, after the third time the Japanese guy responded, "Hot-a-cackie" and then gave them to me.

I was thinking that if I'm in Canada and a Japanese person came up to me at a restaurant where I served pancakes and he ordered "hot-a-cackie," I'm going to understand they want hotcakes, so why was it so different the other way around? It's not that much of a stretch. But these are the things that happen, the experiences you have when you're working overseas, that make them such memorable trips.

It's just culture shock when you're twenty years old

and you don't know anything anyway. Never mind going to all these other countries. I mean, you're in another world all by yourself basically, and you don't know what is going on.

To try and explain our lives to people who aren't in the wrestling business, it's just hard for them to comprehend, they can't believe it. If I told you, "Hey man, here's a hundred dollars Canadian, you're going to Japan, hopefully someone will be at the airport to pick you up. See you in three weeks." How would you react? Most people would be like, "I need a little bit more of a commitment here."

For me, it was fulfilling a dream, I didn't give a damn about commitments. When I first went to Japan I was twenty years old and had only wrestled in thirty-nine matches, so to get a chance to go to Tokyo, Japan, was a lot better than going to Ponoka, Alberta, again to wrestle at the Moose Hall in front of 125 people. And that's all that mattered.

Food

"A blooming onion? I would not like some of your deep-fried ball of onion."
—CHRIS JERICHO

When you're a world-class athlete making a living with your body, you must make sure it is always in great shape. In order to get your physique to look the way you want and perform the way you want, you must give it what it needs.

This means training, but it also means nourishment. WWE Superstars spend quite a bit of time on the road fueling their bodies with the food it needs to remain in peak physical condition. What some of them have found out, though, is that restaurants are not only a great spot to find food, they're also a popular source of entertainment.

Sometimes it's the food and other times it's the person serving the food, but whatever the reason, "food" seems to be in the middle of many of the funniest stories from the road.

Jeet?

Chris Jericho

I've been all over the world thanks to this business. Japan, Mexico, Europe, Australia, all over Canada. You name it, I've been there. One of the toughest places for me to get used to, though, was Tennessee.

The accents were so thick and so strong and so different from what I was used to. It was just a whole other universe to me the first time I went.

You know what j-e-e-t means in Tennessee? Jeet? People will come over and ask you, "Jeet?" I had no idea what they were saying when I first heard it, but I learned that "Jeet" means "Did you eat?"

I've had many conversations in Tennessee like this:

"Jeet?"

"Excuse me, what?"

"Jeet? Y'all . . . jeet?"

"Huh? Jeet? What are you talking about?"

And when it comes to eating, one of the foods that seems to be popular in Tennessee that I'd never heard of is a blooming onion. One day it was explained to me that a blooming onion is a big, fried onion.

"Jeet? No? Y'all like a bloomin' onion?"

"A blooming onion? No, I would not like some of your deep-fried ball of onion."

I also love it when people there tell me they have watched a tape of one of my matches. They refer to it as the V-C-Arrra.

"Hey, Chris Jericho, I saw you rasslin' there on the V-C-Arrra!"

Tennessee. It might be in the United States, but it's on another planet for me.

Want Fries with That protein Shake?

John Cena

Keeping a schedule on the road is definitely tough, especially when you're trying to keep a healthy lifestyle. But on the road I eat whatever I want. If you limit yourself to eating healthy all the time, you're going to starve.

By the time we get out of most shows a lot of stuff isn't open. Rather than feel guilty about what I'm doing, I just kind of eat what I want. I mean, don't get me wrong, I try to eat healthy whenever I can. It's not like I'm scarfing down ice-cream cake and doughnuts all week, but if Waffle House is the only thing open, I'm eating at Waffle House.

If I had my choice and was driving down a road lined with every fast-food place imaginable, Burger King would be my first stop with Taco Bell a close second. It doesn't get much better than a grilled stuffed burrito, but the thing is you can't go back-to-back days with Taco Bell. When I'm at Burger King it's always a Double Whopper with Cheese and nothing else.

Like I said, I don't limit myself with food when I'm on the road. If I'm hungry I'll eat. Now, when I'm home, it's just the opposite, I'm real strict. Living with four other guys we always have steaks in the house, so I'll grill up some of those when the weather lets me. But for the most part it's all protein shakes and meal replacements when I'm back in Massachusetts.

An Expensive Omelet

Jackie Gayda

The morning after our "Three Divas in a Bed" episode (described in Chapter 3), we were scheduled on an early-morning flight to our next show in Wheeling, West Virginia. When Victoria, Gail Kim, and I got outside, we found out right away that the nighttime clerk wasn't kidding about us getting the last room in the place—Bubba Ray Dudley, Rob

Van Dam, and Shane McMahon were out in the parking lot, sleeping in their car.

Sleeping in a car isn't the most comfortable way to spend the night I'm sure, but there are times where it beats the alternative of driving around for a few hours looking for a room when you just have to wake up at sunrise to catch a flight. Sometimes you're just better off grabbing a quick nap in your rental car.

The three guys were waking up as we packed our car, so we all headed off to the airport together. We got there about an hour or so before our flight was set to leave and decided to get some breakfast before heading to the gate. The only thing open was this diner-type place with waitress service. Everyone ordered their eggs and bacon to get some good protein in to start the day.

Gail ordered an omelet. Now the thing with Gail is that she hates cheese of any kind. Absolutely hates it. She must have reminded our waitress three or four times when placing her order, "I don't want any cheese in that omelet, please."

And when the omelet came, what did it have in it? Cheese, of course.

Gail sent it back and waited for a new one. The kitchen didn't exactly rush her order this time. We all waited around with her to finish the cheese-less omelet, thinking we had plenty of time to get to our plane. It was now about thirty minutes before we were set to take off.

There was a little bit of a line at the security check, about ten minutes or so. This was a small terminal, so there was only one line. Gail was the first one through with no problem. Bubba went up next and they decided to check him more on the way through. As they are doing this, no one else can go through the metal detector. We're all stuck behind him.

We told Gail to just go on to the gate, there was no sense in her waiting around. After a couple of minutes checking Bubba's things, they finally moved him aside while they finished and let us make our way through. They checked out a couple of our bags, and made us take our shoes off.

By the time we all got through and gathered our things, it's ten minutes to take off. We finally got to the gate and the agent told us, "Sorry, we close off boarding fifteen minutes before scheduled takeoff."

Close off boarding? She can't be serious. The plane was still at the gate, it hasn't moved. The walkway to get on the plane was still there. The plane's door was still open. We could actually see the inside of the plane and we're not allowed to board? This is incredible.

We asked her a few times to please let us on, pleading our case hoping to get some sympathy. She wouldn't budge. Bubba started arguing with her, pointing out that in the time she spent keeping us off the plane, we could have been on, settled in our seats, and probably already napping. The plane still hadn't moved. We wasted a few more minutes trying to change her mind, but it was useless. They told us they'd have us booked on the next flight, which was set to leave in an hour or so.

Okay, so no big deal, we'll just get there a little bit after we planned. We'd just have to cut our workouts short or something.

About half an hour later, we find out our next flight has been canceled. Not delayed. Canceled. This morning was not going well for us. The only funny thing about all of this was that the five of us who now remained had all sat around at the diner waiting for Gail to finish her omelet, and she was the only one who got to the plane on time.

Fed up with all that's happened to us in the last hour, Bubba decided he was not sitting around the airport anymore waiting for another flight that may or may not ever take off. He told us that he was going to rent a car and drive to Wheeling. Everyone was invited to join him.

The mileage listed on the plane ticket was three hundred, so we figured the drive would take us between four and five hours. A long drive, sure, but we'd still be able to get to the building with a little time to spare. Well, that three hundred miles meant three hundred miles in the air. In a straight line. On the roads it was over four hundred.

We pulled into town just as the show was about to start. Victoria and I had to change into our outfits in the back of the car. We took turns, one changed while the other held up one of the guys shirts as a curtain to block off the view.

When we finally got to the building, Victoria and I went right over to talk to Gail, who had probably gotten in a workout at the gym and a nice nap while we were driving four hundred miles through the West Virginia countryside. Pulling off one of our best all-time acting jobs, the two of us walked up to her like we were all mad.

"From now on, if they put cheese in your omelet, you are going to eat the omelet. There's no more sending it back."

Many I Take Your Order

Al Snow

When we get out of shows it's sometimes tough to find a place to eat. Most of the time we're forced to stop at the drive-through of a fast-food place in the middle of nowhere. An interesting thing about these places at that time of night is that they don't actually expect too many customers, so they'll stick just about anyone in that window. And for some reason, these people are always more fun to mess around with.

One night I was riding with two other Superstars, one man and one woman. As we drove up to the place, we thought of a great practical joke to pull on the drive-through attendant. We got some rope, duct tape, and a blanket and stuck the chick in the backseat. We put the rope around her, the duct tape on her mouth, and the blanket on top.

We go to the microphone and order the food like normal. When we pull up to pay and pick up the food, the guy's looking out the window and sees something struggling in the backseat. All of a sudden the blanket comes off and there's a woman all tied up in the backseat with duct tape on her mouth.

I immediately turn around and yell at her, "Stop moving! I told you next time you'll be in the trunk!" Then I looked at the attendant and told him, "You didn't see anything, all right?"

We drove off real fast and didn't even wait to see if the cops came after us. We went right to the hotel. The guy in the counter was speechless, stunned. "Uhhh . . . Uhhhh." It was great

Losing My Lunch

Big Show

I'm driving with Billy Gunn in Pittsburgh and we're running late. We stopped at the gym, stopped to go tanning, and before we knew it, only had time to grab drive-through food because we had to get to the building quickly.

It's Pittsburgh, so there's traffic regardless of the day or time. We merge on to this big highway that has four lanes of traffic. As we merge in, this guy from two lanes over swerves and cuts us right off. Billy blows the horn to say, "Hey buddy, there's someone behind ya."

There's three people in the car and the guy in the backseat looks through the rear window and flips us the bird.

Now, they're driving forty, fifty miles an hour down the road and thought they were invincible. I hate it when people think they are safe in a car and grow these huge balls and start to think, "I'm so tough because no one can touch me." It just really bothers me. They show no respect for anyone else.

I just snap when I see that finger go up. I immediately open the door while we're still going fifty miles an hour and step out with one foot on the hood. I'm holding the handrail with my left hand and I have my right foot out in front of me, on the hood. With my right hand I reach into the bag and take out the triple cheeseburger I'd just gotten from Wendy's. Their car is only maybe six feet in front of our hood so I gun the cheeseburger at them and splatter it all over their rear window.

Billy and I were cracking up.

Then it dawned on me that it took me about three seconds to get out here, I had done it without even thinking. Now my ass is hanging out of a car going fifty miles an hour down a highway, how am I going to get back in?

Then I started to wonder what these other people must be thinking. There's a cheeseburger splattered all over their rear window and a five-hundred-pound giant pretending to be a hood ornament on the car behind them. They're looking back and seeing a monster hanging out of the car, who they think is going to do a Jackie Chan and jump on their hood or something because they got right off the highway at the next exit.

Billy slowed down a bit and let me sink my way back in. The worst part about the whole thing is, after I finally got myself back in the car, I realized I threw my lunch out.

Tossing the cheeseburger at them was funny, but probably not worth it. I was starving by the time we got to the building.

Don't Expect a Tip

Sergeant Slaughter

The night Vince McMahon talked to me about turning my character against America, I agreed to do it. He appreciated my enthusiasm and team-first attitude, but asked me to take some time to think it over and speak with my wife about it.

"This will change your life," he told me.

I knew he was right; if this angle worked as well as we all thought it might, my life would not be the same. I just had no idea how much and how quickly the change would hit.

One of the first nights we did the heel turn was at a Pay-Per-View in Miami. After the show I was in one of the taping rooms finishing up my promos, when they replayed an interview "Mean" Gene Okerlund did with the Ultimate Warrior earlier in the night. Midway through the promo, Gene just stopped, put his finger to his ear like someone was talking to him on his earpiece. He looked at the camera and said, "Hold on, hold on. Well, I can't believe it. I can't believe what I've just been told. . . . I regret to inform you that Sgt. Slaughter has just desecrated the American flag."

As I'm hearing Gene say this, I didn't think much of it at the time. I laughed it off. Little did I know that comment was going to make it very rough for me after that point—starting that very night.

I went right from the building to a Denny's or an IHOP-type place in the area with a friend of mine who lived outside Miami. The two of us were just about the only people in the restaurant at this hour. We decided what we wanted and were waiting to order. No one came to help us. There was a man who looked like he worked there, standing in the back near the kitchen with his head down, but he wasn't coming over to us. We waited some more. Still no one came. And a little bit more. Finally, my friend yells out, "Can we please get a waitress or someone to help us here. We'd like to eat."

The guy picked up his head, and the first thing you

could see is that he had a big Marine Corps tattoo on his shoulder. He looked over to us and pointed at my friend, "You can eat, but he can't."

We laughed, assuming he was kidding around with us. He wasn't. He had watched the show and didn't like what he heard.

The two of us had to leave. The only other thing open at that hour was a 7-Eleven up the road. I ate a few hot dogs and called it a night.

Stuff like this happened often to me while I was playing the "bad" Sgt. Slaughter. I got used to three-hot-dog dinners on the go.

Manopac

Croton Falls

11

100

684

20

21

4   WOOSTER
MTN. ST. PK.

12

North
Salem

121

7

8

8

Somers

8

Purdys

116

West
Redding

53

202

7

Tibcus
Res.

121

Waccabuc
Lake

116

10

7

Red

Goldens
Bridge

138

124

South
Salem

35

Ridge-
field

6

35

22

35

Cross
River

35

123

102

Branch

124

33

Streets
Pond

5

35

6

Katonah

New
Croton
Res.

13

Bedford
Hills

121

137

River

Cross

124

Trinity
Lake

123

8

Can-
da

Mt.
Kisco

117

4

172

Bedford

Pound Ridge

North
Wilton

123

Wilton

1

7

10

22

Laurel
Res.

137

124

S. Norwalk
Res.

3

ap-
qua

684

Banksville

Long
Ridge

New
Canaan

Silvermine R.

3

nt-

Converse
Pd.

104

North
Stamford

3

W

Armonk

Stanwich

Norwalk

Round
Hill

Rockwood
Lake

29

15

PKWY.

5

36

37

6

1

8

31

106

5

4

12

10

Putnam
Lake

Darien

136

N

2

28

Mianus
Cos
Cob

137

11

Rowa

120

Glenville

95

10

Noroton

Rye
Lake

27

3

9

LODGE

4

Stamford

INTRACOAST

te

Greenwich

11

2

3

5

Old Greenwich

Riverside

as

287

BRUCE
MUSEUM

23

Harrison

Byram

Port
Chester

20

2

127

21

Rye

4

Mamaroneck

1

LON

ten

The Bathroom

"I was about three inches from having an ass full of porcelain and having to call the office and try to explain that one."

—BIG SHOW

When there's eating and drinking, there's got to be bathroom stops. Big Show shares his fondest restroom memories.

A giant Shit Fit

Big Show

I did something quite strange the first time I was in Japan to work. 💠 I was with WCW at the time, and we flew straight from Atlanta to Japan. It took something like sixteen, seventeen hours in the air, and then we jumped right on a bus for a two-hour ride to the hotel that was somewhere outside of Tokyo.

There aren't many details about the hotel I remember, but one thing I'll never forget is that it was massive. I can't remember the name of it, the exact city it was in, nothing like that other than how big a building it was. It was a business hotel. Meaning it was a place for Japanese businessmen to sleep, shower, and go to their meeting. A five-hundred-pound guy in town for a wrestling show wasn't the target clientele of this place.

A couple of us were staying in rooms right near each other and had to take the elevator up to somewhere on the seventieth floor to get there.

When I got off the elevator, the first thing I noticed was that there were like a hundred rooms in every direction you looked. I figured out the way to my room and started walking. Now, we're staying in Japan for a week, so I got all these heavy bags I'm pulling behind me. I'm real tired from all the traveling and I feel like I'm walking through a maze. This wasn't the happiest moment of my life.

I had to drag on through this hallway forever because my room turned out to be the last door. Lex Luger was staying right across the hall from me and we were figuring we must have walked for at least a hundred yards to get to the rooms from the elevator. I'm not kidding you, it was about the length of a football field.

Now, when I'm on a flight for that long, the first thing I always do when I get to my room is go to the bathroom. I have to get in there and free myself up. After almost a full day of traveling, I'm excited when I finally get to the door just to be somewhere with a bed and a toilet to use. I swing the door open and do not like what I see. There was literally, maybe, two feet of room from where the door opened to the bed.

And the bed was just about pushed to the walls on all four sides. I could have practically touched the back wall standing there in the doorway. There was barely enough room between the foot of the bed and the dresser for a normal-sized person to walk, forget about me. This was going to be a tough trip.

Well, I step on in figuring there's nothing I can do about the size of the room right now. I shut the front door and notice that the bathroom was behind where the main door had opened so I didn't notice it until now.

The bathroom door was about half as wide and a foot or so shorter than regular doors I was used to. The bathroom itself was maybe six feet by five and a half feet with both a bathtub and a toilet in it. To call this bathroom small is an understatement. It was really more like a Port-o-Potty than an actual bathroom.

But I really had to go.

It didn't take long for me to realize that because I'm seven-feet-two and the toilet is tiny and not very far off the ground, I won't be able to sit on it, especially with the wall built right in front of it. One knee would be pressed up against my face and the other would be jammed into the wall. The big issue was that I had already geared myself up to go to the bathroom and now it's like trying to hold back the flood waters of time while I'm deciding if there's a way to get on this toilet without injuring myself.

I *really* had to go.

As I leaned up against the wall with my foot resting on the toilet trying to figure out my options I had a jet-lag-fueled temper tantrum.

I took my left arm and swung it against the wall about

as hard as I could. These walls were very thin and put up in big sections attached to one another with bolts. When I hit the one panel I knocked all the bolts out of it and a four-foot section of wall fell back right out into the hallway. The quick renovations allowed me to fit on the toilet without having to sit with my head between my knees.

Now you've got this huge hole in the wall with a five-hundred-pound guy sitting on the toilet with half his ass hanging out in the hallway of this Japanese business hotel. It wasn't the most flattering sight, but it was the only thing that would work for me.

I *really* had to go.

One of the other boys came walking by heading into Lex's room while I was mid-shit, looked at me, shook his head, and asked, "Giant shit fit?"

I always thought that was a great line.

Risky Business

Big Show

A few years ago I went over to India to do a promotional tour for WWE. I'd never been there, so I was curious to see it but was real paranoid about some health issues.

We had to get like twelve shots before we went over. I was worried about eating the food over there and also brought like eight cases of bottled water with me. I was all about the bottled water during this trip. I'm drinking bottled water, I'm brushing my teeth with bottled water, showering with bottled water. That's right, I was doing the Hollywood movie star, Evian bath.

It might have been a bit much, but I didn't trust the water. I didn't want it in my eyes, didn't want to risk swallowing it or have it get into any open cuts. I didn't want to pick up any disease I wouldn't be able to get rid of or fall over dead two days into the trip. That wouldn't have been good.

So we get to our hotel and have a little bit of time before we have to head out for the first appearance. I was traveling with the guy from the promotional company who takes great care of us on these trips and we decided to go to our rooms to drop all of our stuff off before we left. Between my luggage and water I had tons of stuff to get into the room.

This wasn't a regular room I was staying in, either. WWE put me in a huge suite. That's one thing I love about WWE, it knows how to take care of its talent.

With the little bit of time I had, I figured I'd take care of business in the bathroom. Now this suite had these elaborate European-style toilets that came out of the wall. They were nice from a decoration standpoint, but not practical. They had absolutely no support underneath them because they were built right into the wall. I guess a luxurious suite in a classy Indian hotel doesn't get many five-hundred-pound guests.

As soon as I saw the set up of these things I knew it would be risky for a guy my size, but nature was calling so I didn't have a choice. I had to get on.

I'm sitting down for a little while, reading my golf magazine and everything is comfortable, everything is great.

Now remember, I'd only been in the room for a few minutes so I didn't know much about it yet. One of things I wasn't familiar with was the sound of the doorbell.

It was so friggin' loud. It was like a bomb siren going off.

Ding . . . dong! Ding . . . dong!

It just echoed through the entire suite. I thought there was a speaker in the bathroom or something, it was so loud. When it blasted through the suite I really had no idea what it was.

Ding . . . dong! Ding . . . dong!

This bell caught me so off guard that as soon as it rang through the suite I jumped up off the toilet and ripped it right out of the wall when I crashed back down on it.

As it's crumbling under me I somehow managed to hold myself up by grabbing the sink with my right hand and the towel rack with my left. I look down and see there's all this broken porcelain and everything else below me. I started to think about how I was so nervous about the food and the water and now I was so close to falling in this mess.

I was about three inches from having an ass full of porcelain and having to call the office and try to explain that one.

I pushed off the sink to get back on my feet and get the hell out of there. We went right to the appearance for four hours and when we got back there was already a new toilet on the wall.

I pity the poor maintenance guy who had to make that call.

Fishkill
Newburgh
Beacon
FISHKILL MTNS.
APPALACHIAN TRAIL
Hudson
Vails Gate
Cornwall-on-Hudson
Cornwall
Gold Spring
West Point
Mountainville
WEST POINT
MIL. ACAD. RES.
Garrison
Highland Falls
Ft. Montgomery
Holmes
Lake Carmel
Kent Cliff
Roaring Brook Lake
W. Branch Res.
Lake Secor
Tompkins Corners
Mahopac Falls
Mahopac
Croton Falls
TACONIC
STATE
Shrub Oak
Mohegan Lake
Jefferson Valley
Somers
Goldens Bridge
Peekskill
Jones Point
Bear Mtn.
Yorktown Heights
Amawalk
Katonah
Buchanan
Montrose
Tomkins Cove
Stony Point
W. Haverstraw
Haverstraw
Croton-on-Hudson
Millwood
Mt. Kisco
Bedford Hills
PALISADES
INTERSTATE PKWY.
Mt. Ivy
Ossining
Chappaqua
Congers
New City
Briarcliff Manor
Pleasantville
Spring Valley
Scarborough
N. Tarrytown
Hawthorne
Armonk
Nyack
Nanuet
Tarrytown
Valhalla
Montvale
Pearl River
Piermont
Irvington
Elmsford
Tappan
Sparkill
Dobbs Ferry
Ardsley
White Plains
SAW MILL RIVER
THWY.
N.Y.
N.J.
CONN.
GARDEN STATE PKWY.
Round Hill

The author would like to thank all of the Superstars who shared

their road stories with him. He'd also like to confess that he lis-

tened very closely as Victoria explained to him how she ended

up in bed with Jackie Gayda and Gail Kim one night. He also

learned more about the Big Show's bathroom habits than any

person should.

Miraculously, none of the Superstars locked him in a car

trunk during the journey, and for this he is grateful.